C000172540

Tempus
Two in One Series

SUTTON COLDFIELD

Tempus
Two in One Series

SUTTON COLDFIELD

Compiled by
Marian Baxter

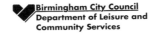
Birmingham City Council
Department of Leisure and
Community Services

TEMPUS

This edition first published 2001
Copyright © Marian Baxter, 2001

Tempus Publishing Limited
The Mill, Brimscombe Port,
Stroud, Gloucestershire, GL5 2QG

ISBN 0 7524 2213 8

Typesetting and origination by
Tempus Publishing Limited
Printed in Great Britain by
Midway Clark Printing, Wiltshire

Originally produced as two books:

Sutton Coldfield
First published 1994
Copyright © Marian Baxter, 1994
ISBN 0 7524 0043 6

Sutton Coldfield: The Second Selection
First published 1997
Copyright © Marian Baxter, 1997
ISBN 0 7524 1070 9

IMAGES
of England

SUTTON COLDFIELD

Compiled by
Marian Baxter

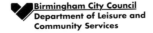

Birmingham City Council
Department of Leisure and
Community Services

TEMPUS

Contents

Acknowledgements

My thanks go to Birmingham City Council,
Department of Leisure and Community Services, Libraries and Learning,
for allowing me to use their photographs.

Thanks to Martin Flynn,
Faculty Manager of Local Studies and History, Birmingham Central Library,
who did the negotiations with the publisher
and encouraged me to put this volume together.

Special thanks to Mrs Trisha Baugh and Mrs Margaret Goodger
for typing the manuscript.

In addition I wish to thank the staff of Sutton Coldfield Reference Library
for their help and advice in selecting the photographs.

Introduction

Sutton Coldfield lies approximately seven miles north-east of Birmingham, eight miles from Lichfield, seven miles from Tamworth, and seven miles from Coleshill. The boundary in the south-east corner is formed by the River Tame. Just below 250 feet above sea level, but most of the area between 250 and 450 feet, with higher ground to the north and east rising to 568 feet and another 1,500 from green belt along the eastern side. It is the most northerly constituency of Birmingham and borders Staffordshire and Warwickshire countryside to the north and east.

The Royal Town of Sutton Coldfield is an ancient town, once forming part of the kingdom of Mercia. Before the Conquest its wood and chase provided sport for the Mercian earls as they did for the subsequent royalty and nobility until the time of Bishop Vesey in the Tudor period. The *Domesday Book* entry for Sutton Coldfield, the first known written mention of the town, describes the 1,000 acres of arable land as having "22 ploughs", ten acres of meadow, woodland two leagues long and one league wide, and when exploited, its value was thirty shillings. The value of the Manor was four pounds and it was held by Edwin, Earl of Mercia, for the King.

Under the Earls of Warwick, Sutton Coldfield thrived. It held a weekly market and an annual fair, and for a time Sutton market was one of the most important in the district. Sutton Coldfield became a royal manor in 1489 and remained in the hands of the crown until 1528 when through Bishop Vesey Henry VIII granted the town its first Charter of Incorporation. The Charter decreed that the 'town and village shall be for ever here-after be accounted, named and called the Royal Town of Sutton Coldfield'. A corporation of twenty-five men known as the 'Warden and Society' was created with all manorial rights, powers and liberties.

The Corporation of Sutton Coldfield recorded its appreciation of Bishop Vesey in 1533 in these words, 'Through his own efforts and at his own expense, he has transformed Sutton from a poor, ruinous country place into a flourishing and prosperous town, and he has bestowed houses and cattle on the people here, who had been completely destitute before'.

Over the years there were many accusations by the inhabitants of the abuse of privileges and misuse of funds. In spite of Bishop Vesey's attempts to turn Sutton into thriving town, it retained its rural character until the last century, when its popularity as a residential area for people working in the neighbouring industrial town began to give its present character. Sutton Coldfield's attempt to become industrious took place in the late seventeenth and early eighteenth centuries, when most of the pools in Sutton park were formed by damming the streams, and mills were built on them. Their trades ranged from buttons, leather, bayonet and blade to cotton making. However, with the growth of industry in Birmingham and the surrounding towns the water-powered industry soon found itself unable to compete. The Corporation became extinct in 1885 when, after a Royal Commission had been set up to enquire into unreformed boroughs, the Municipal Corporation Act of 1882 established a uniform system of borough government. In 1886 a new Charter was granted. The properties of the Corporation were handed over to a new Council and the town was divided into six wards and represented by six aldermen and eighteen councillors. The first mayor of Sutton Coldfield was J. Benjamin Stone, the well-known photographer, many of whose photographs appear in this book. The population of Sutton Coldfield was then under 8,000.

The administration of the Borough Council continued without serious challenge until the early 1970s when Local Government reorganisation proposed to move Sutton Coldfield from the County of Warwickshire into the Metropolitan District of Birmingham. On 1 April 1974 Sutton Coldfield became the largest constituency in the Metropolitan District of Birmingham, covering just over one fifth of Birmingham's administrative area.

Much of Sutton is open space with the 2,400 acres of Sutton park, the proposed New Hall Valley Country Park, as well as most of the City's Green Belt provide the Constituency with one of its major assets, Sutton Park, and site of special local interest under the Wildlife and Countryside Act of 1981, is the largest Local Authority Park of its type within the United kingdom. It is a remnant of an extensive forest that formerly covered much of the Midlands area, and contains some of the last surviving examples of natural countryside in that area. The Park's natural features, the richness and diversity of its wildlife, together with a colourful history, combine to make it a site of national importance. There are three main elements of the landscape, namely Woodland, Wetland, and Heathland. It is made more remarkable by its complete encirclement by suburban development, making it a sanctuary for many kinds of plants, insects, animals and birds, including some species which are scarce in the west midlands region. The town centre is the second largest shopping centre in the city and a major suburban office centre. There are also comprehensive shopping centres in each of the highly residential areas of Boldmere, Mere Green and Wlyde Green.

Sutton Coldfield is a mainly residential area and industry is confined to light and service industries. The total population of Sutton Coldfield based on the 1991 census returns was 90,325 with a total population for Birmingham persons resident on the night of the census being 961,041. The population of Sutton Coldfield accounts for approximately 9 per cent of the total of Birmingham. In acreage Sutton Coldfield accounts for approximately 21 per cent of that of Birmingham.

Housing is by far the major land use in the built up area, reflecting the rapid population growth in recent years (an 80 per cent growth between 1851 and 1981). The wide range of housing reflects the character and high quality found in this Birmingham constituency.

Sutton Coldfield Central library is unique in that apart from the Birmingham Central Library it houses Lending, Children's, Music, Reference and Local Studies departments. The Local Studies Department houses some 112,000 items relating to the Sutton Coldfield area.

Of the department's collection of photographs relating to the area, numbering 4,500, over 200 have been selected for this first-ever published collection of photographs relating solely to Sutton Coldfield. This fascinating collection of images of Sutton Coldfield's history and its people have been taken from the nationally famous photographer J. Benjamin Stone to the amateur view taken by the person next door.

The Local Studies Department is always seeking to add to its collection both in knowledge and in additional photographic material. If people have unwanted photographs of the area the department is always willing to give them a good home where their unique information can be shared with others.

One
Wylde Green

The Sutton Coldfield town sign on the Birmingham/Sutton Coldfield boundary, 1938. Sutton Coldfield was granted the right to be called a Royal Town under a charter granted by Henry VIII in 1528.

Wylde Green House, 1907. This magnificent house stood on the Birmingham Road near Wylde Green Road. The house has now gone but the lodge still stands today.

Boys from Wylde Green College on the playing fields, 1927. The College was established in 1922 by Frederick Burd as a private boys' school, and is situated on the Birmingham Road.

The Post Office, Wylde Green, stood on the corner of Birmingham Road and Wylde Green Road, seen here in 1892.

Cottages on Sutton Road opposite Monkseaton Road, 1892.

James Conchar, a native of Crossmichael, Scotland, resided in Wylde Green in 1873. Having been, in his youth, much connected with farming, Mr Conchar in 1882 rented two farms in Wylde Green where he kept a small stud of shire and hackney horses. He was the Mayor of Sutton Coldfield in 1892-1893. This photo shows Mr Conchar's Stud Farm, on the lane at the back of Wylde Green House (Wylde Green Road), 1907.

Cottages on the Birmingham Road, Wylde Green, 1892.

Two
Boldmere

The Beggars Bush, *c.* 1880. According to legend a beggar is said to have died under the bush. Unfortunately, as the bush marked the parish boundary there was a dispute as to who should pay the cost of the burial. The bush situated on the Chester Road was dug up in the early 1930s when the road was widened.

The Beggars Bush Public House, 1907.

Old Cottages on the corner of Gravelly Lane and Chester Road. The cottages were demolished to make way for the Pavilion Cinema. Closed in the early 1960s for conversion to a ten-pin bowling alley, it was demolished in 1974.

The Gate Inn, Boldmere Road, which was demolished and replaced by the Boldmere Public House, 1938.

Boldmere Infants School, Boldmere Road, March 1938.

Three
Maney

Horse and carriage on Wyndley Lane, January 1893.

The Horse and Jockey Public House on the corner of Jockey Road, 1892.

The White House at Maney was demolished in 1935 to make way for the Odeon Cinema. It was at the White House that Doctor Bodingron had his Sanatorium, where he put his advanced medical theories into practice.

Driffold House. Doctor Bodington's claim to fame stems from a paper he wrote in 1840 entitled an *Essay on the treatment and cure of pulmonary consumption*. He spent much of his time caring for the mentally sick at the Driffold House Asylum which stood on the corner of Wyndley Lane and the Driffold.

The Stone House, Maney. Of the fifty-one stone houses built by Bishop Vesey in Tudor times, this Vesey Cottage built of the local sandstone is the largest of the surviving cottages. This picture dates from 1940.

The gardens of The Smithy at the junction of the Driffold and Birmingham Road, *c*. 1946. The gardens were relaid in 1953 and named Bodington Gardens as a memorial to Dr George Bodington.

Cottages at Maney Corner, *c*. 1892. Shakespeare Cottage on the left has not changed, but Vesey Grange on the left had been redesigned and another floor added by 1950.

Vesey Manor, built in the local sandstone, *c*. 1530, was originally built as two properties. Today the owners of Vesey Manor specialise in the selling of antiques. This photograph was taken in 1893.

Installation of a painted predestrian crossing on the Birmingham Road outside the Cottage Hospital, 1938.

The Cup Inn, *c*. 1890. One of Sutton Coldfield's older licensed houses, the present building was erected around the turn of the century. The building in the picture was an earlier single storey building, the landlady being a Mrs Ellery.

Martha and Harriet Baguley's Ladies' School, Manor Road, *c*. 1885-88.

Holland House, the home of the Oughtons, whose mill produced gun barrels, stood on the site of the present Plantsbrook School. It was demolished in 1936.

Maney, *c.* 1910. This may be the Trinity Monday procession.

The Birmingham Road looking towards The Parade.

Maney Post Office and Birmingham Road looking towards The Parade, c. 1890.

Four
Sutton Coldfield Centre

The Parade from the bridge over the Ebrook.

The Parade, c. 1860, looking towards Mill Street. In 1826 a piece of new road was constructed between the Manor Hill and Sutton in order to obtain a more direct line for the turnpike road. The stone dam of the ancient pools was removed, the road remaining still bore the name of The Dam.

The Old Pie Shop stood on the corner of Manor Road and The Parade. It was demolished in 1913. A notice at the bottom of the four steps which led to the entrance read 'Bend or Bump'.

Installation of a painted pedestrian crossing on The Parade, near Queen Street, 1938.

The Parade and the corner of Newhall Street. The Wesleyan Chapel was built in 1887 as a lasting reminder of Queen Victoria's Golden Jubilee celebrations. Opened on 2 April 1888, the building cost £1,675. It was converted into Sutton Coldfield's public library in 1937.

Opposite: Built as a photographers for Speight in 1907, 95 The Parade was to become the MEB showrooms. Used by Booksale Books in the early 1990s, the whole area is due for redevelopment in the mid-1990s. From a picture taken in 1907.

The Parade and Lower Parade, *c.* 1869.

Yew Tree Cottage, Lower Parade. Originally a half timbered house, it measured eighteen feet by twenty-five feet. In 1851 a shoemaker lived here with his family of seven. It was demolished to make way for South Parade.

The Parade and Lower Parade, *c.* 1870. In 1870 the Gothic style front of Town School, now the Baptist Church, still looks much as it does today.

The Old Dog Public House stood at right angles to The Parade, and had stables and a bowling alley, as well as a pigsty and cowhouses. In December 1931 a one-way traffic system was introduced whereby traffic from Mill Street came down Lower Parade to avoid traffic congestion.

The Parade and Lower Parade in winter, 1887. In 1892 a group of shop keepers on The Parade were taken to court for not clearing snow from in front of their shops. On 17 January after a snowfall during the night the defendants had not cleared the pavement by 12 noon as they were required to do, although it had been cleared by Monday morning. The case was dismissed.

Lower Parade *c.* 1895. Originally the Dog was called 'The Talbot' after a breed of hunting dog used for burrowing, so it was often spoken of as The Dog in the hole or The Old Dog. It was renamed The Knott in 1981.

The Empress Cinema, 1935. Work on the building of the cinema started in 1922 and it opened in 1923. Sound was installed in 1927, so Suttonians were able to hear Al Johnson in Sonny Boy. The cinema closed in 1971 and was demolished to make way for the Sainsbury Centre.

The Parade and Lower Parade, *c.* 1900. In 1879 an article in the local newspaper appeared 'In the circular of an entertaining tradesman just issued, the Dam at Sutton is styled The Parade'. The new name of The Parade began to find favour with tradespeople and on 15 May 1880 the first advertisement appeared in the Sutton news for a shop on 'The Parade'.

By 1900 the coming of the telephone was under discussion and in 1901 Ann Higgs, the fruiterers shop on The Parade, had telephone number 1X1. At a cost of £36,000 electric lighting was also to arrive in Sutton.

Longmores on The Parade.

40

The Parade, Sutton Coldfield

The Parade.

Lower Parade and Victoria Road during Queen Victoria's Jubilee Celebrations.

Park Road looking to The Parade and Mill Street, c. 1900.

Park Road. Built and paid for by Sir Edmund Hartop of Four Oaks Hall. Many of the houses served as boarding houses for the increasing number of tourists who spent holidays in Sutton Coldfield.

View from The Manor looking to The Parade, formerly The Dam, *c.* 1870.

The Parade and Mill Street, *c.* 1888. The first building to be erected on The Parade was the Museum Public House. In the 1870s visitors to the public house were provided with a sandwich and a glass of ale for threepence, plain teas for eightpence, or with ham and beef, one shilling. The museum contained a large collection of birds, animals and reptiles, and there were gardens with summer arbours and a large green for dancing.

Alms Houses and the Town Hall. Sutton Coldfield's Town Hall was built in 1859. It was used as such until 1906. It is known today as the Masonic Buildings. It was Sutton's first picture house *c.* 1915, when it was known as Rosella's Cinema. The Almshouses were demolished in 1924, when new ones were opened at Walmley.

The Shand Mason Fire Engine outside the first fire station at the old Town Hall in Mill Street, *c.* 1886.

Sutton Coldfield Volunteer Fire Brigade and the Merryweather steamer outside the new first station. Captain Browning is on the left, *c.* 1905.

Official opening of the fire station, King Edward Square, 1 December 1905.

Mill Street. Named after the early Mill which stood at the top of The Parade. The Emmanuel College Arms Public House on the left was later converted into the main post office. The frontage was preserved and incorporated in the modern building, Emmanual Court, in 1989.

Blind Hill, now known as Trinity Hill, *c*. 1800.

Church Hill, May 1895. Grove Cottage can be distinguished on the door lintel of No. 3. The illuminated sign by No. 8 refers to the 'Old Sun'.

Church Hill, 1906. Originally the Church Hill houses formed a community which occupied the whole of the present Vesey Gardens, consisting of several houses, shops, and two public houses.

50

Mill Street, 1930, showing property demolished in 1936 to make way for Vesey Gardens. No. 1 Church Hill and Mill Street showing the start of demolition in 1936, to make way for Vesey Gardens.

Old Cottages, Church Hill. The courtyard at the rear of the cottages before the buildings were demolished to make way for the Vesey Memorial Gardens.

Mill Street and Coleshill Street: demolition of buildings to make way for Vesey Gardens, 1938.

High Street from Coleshill Road.

Opposite: High Street from the new Vesey Gardens, 1938.

The Stocks have room for three offenders to be secured at a time, and the post at one end is extended to serve as a whipping post or pillory. In 1787 Richard Ball was found guilty of stealing a wagon rope and a plank and sentenced to be stripped to the waist and whipped until his body was bloody. This re-enactment is from 1895.

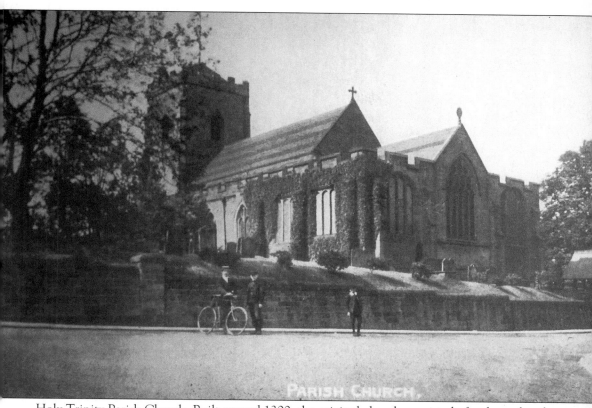

Holy Trinity Parish Church. Built around 1300, the original church consisted of a chancel and a nave. In the 1500s under Bishop Vesey's control it was extended by two aisles and the tower was added. Extensions in the eighteenth and nineteenth centuries together with another small extension in 1930 give us Holy Trinity Church as it looks today.

Sutton Coldfield Church, 1891, the Nave and Chancel.

Pudsey and Vesey Monuments, 1895. The Pudsey monument is on the left and the Bishop Vesey monument is in the corner. The east window dates from 1530, the stained glass by Ballantine of Edinburgh was put in around 1870.

Beneath lie the Remains of that pious and learned Prelate JOHN HERMAN als VESEY who was promoted by KING HENRY in
the 8ᵗʰ in yᵗʰ year of This Reign to yᵉ See of Exeter, was employed by Him on sundry Embassies, was Tutor to his then only Daughter
the Lady MARY & President of Wales.
So great was his Affection for this his native place yᵗ he spared neither Cost nor Pains to improve it and make it flourish
He procured it to be incorporate by the Name of a Warden and Society of the Kings Town of Sutton Coldfield & procured to them
their Successors for ever the Chase, Park and Manor.
He built two Isles to yᵉ Church, and an Organ, erected yᵉ Moot Hall with a Prison under it and a Market place, gave to them the Profits
improvement of Youth, founded &endowed a Free Grammar School, which was rebuilt A.D.1728.
two stone Bridges, one at Curdworth & one at Watertorton, paved yᵉ whole Town, gave a Meadow to poor Widows, & for the
his Munificence, and died in yᵉ 103ᵈ Year of his Age and in the Year of our Lord M.D.LV.
He built Moor Hall, where He spent yᵉ latter Part of his Life in Hospitality & Sᵗ Job ever for many Years spent the
This Monument erected by JOHN WYRLEY of Hampsted in Handsworth, & a Relation & one of ye SUCCESSOR of this
Bishop his Great Uncle, was repaired and beautified by This Corporation in yᵉ Year of our Lord 17...

Bishop Vesey's Monument, 1895. The Vesey Tomb is placed directly over a vault containing the Bishop's remains. The inscription at the base describes Bishop Vesey as 'John Harman or Vesey who died in his 103rd year 1555'. It is thought, however, that his age has been exaggerated and that his birth was not in 1452 but rather 1462. He is shown wearing pre-reformation vestments which would have been compulsory under Queen Mary (1553-58) but forbidden in the reign of Elizabeth I (1558-1603), which suggests that the effigy was carved shortly after his death. The wording on the tomb extols the virtues of the Bishop, and lists the many benefits which he brought about for the Royal Town of Sutton Coldfield and he is remembered with gratitude.

Mary Ashford's gravestone, 1895, Holy Trinity Churchyard. On 27 May 1817 the body of Mary Ashford was discovered in a marl pit near Penns Lane, for which Abraham Thornton was arrested, tried and acquitted. The grave stone standing in Holy Trinity Church read as follows: 'As a warning to female virtue and a humble monument to female chastity, this stone marks the grave of Mary Ashford, who in the 20th year of her age, having incautiously repaired to a sense of amusement without proper protection, was brutally violated and murdered on 27 May 1817 … ' Many people still believe even today that Mary's death was accidental, so it remains one of Sutton Coldfield's unsolved murders.

Dawney Tomb, Holy Trinity churchyard. Thomas Dawney, a member of a Yorkshire family and later raised to the peerage under the title of Viscount Downe, lived in the Manor House in Sutton. He died in 1671 and was buried in Holy Trinity Churchyard and left in his will a dole of bread 'for which the attendance of claimants broke down the floor of Vesey's original Moot Hall'.

Coleshill Street, 1950.

Victoria's Jubilee Dispensary, Coleshill Street, *c*. 1955. Founded in 1888, by the following year 1,279 people were subscribing to the Dispensary and receiving medicine and medical attention. The Dispensary stayed open until 1948 when the National Health Act came into force.

Corner of Coleshill Street and Trinity Hill. Cottages demolished 1959.

Rectory Road looking up to the top at Coleshill Street, 1955.

Winter scene from Mrs Jerrome's of Holland House looking towards Coleshill Road.

Kings Arms, Coleshill Road, an old coaching house. It was rebuilt shortly before the Second World War.

Trinity Hill looking to Coleshill Street, 1895.

Mill Street looking down towards The Parade.

Mill Street, *c.* 1890.

Coleshill Street looking towards High Street. The Old Sun was demolished in 1936 to make way for Vesey Gardens.

Mill Street, 1887. The Royal Oak Inn was demolished to make way for the Vesey Gardens in 1937. At 10.00am one Tuesday night Mr George Edward Stanier, tenant of the Royal Oak Hotel, called 'Time gentlemen please'. The next day the full license of the house was transferred to the New Oscott Tavern, Chester Road.

Pepper Pot Weighing Machine. View looking down the High Street towards the Parish Church. The buildings in front of Holy Trinity Church were demolished in 1938 to make way for the Vesey Memorial Gardens. The Pepper Pot was a public weighing machine. The metal place on which the carts stood is just behind the man on the left. The charges for weighing were: wagons fourpence and carts twopence.

Trinity Monday, *c.* 1887. Trinity Monday was the fair day when the fair was proclaimed at the town Hall by the Deputy Steward, supported by the Sergeant-at-Mace, the Town Crier, and a number of the oldest men, the latter carrying pikes or halberds and marching in the High Street and back to the Town Hall where they were dismissed, each man receiving a sum of money. The proclamation was made until the old Warden and Society ceased to exist in 1886. The Carnival continued in Sutton Coldfield until the 1930s.

High Street. Many of the buildings in the High Street appear on the statutory list of historical buildings. Vesey House on the right used to be the home of Agnes Bracken, the author of the first history of Sutton, the *History of the Forest and Chase of Sutton Coldfield*, written in 1860. The front has been considerably altered for use as shop premises.

High Street, 1904.

High Street.

High Street. The Lord Leigh mentioned in the banner was appointed High Steward to the town in 1859. The town celebrates his visit.

High Street, celebrating Lord Leigh's visit to Sutton Coldfield.

High Street, 1870. The black and white timbered cottages were removed to make Railway Road (Blue Brick Street) and the London and North Western Railway Tunnel on the Lichfield line. The building next to timbered buildings is known as Ennis House.

High Street, 1887. The history of the Three Tuns Public House goes back to medieval times. It was standing during the War of the Roses and during the Civil War — it is reputed that Cromwell stayed here. The present, late eighteenth-century structure covers earlier foundations and cellars.

Ivy House, High Street, c. 1886.

Midland Drive from the rear of Ivy House. Town Station is just visible through the trees on the right, 1898.

The Old Swan Hotel, later the Royal, 1880. The Swan Inn is the present Royal Hotel. The building dates back to c. 1750. It was a private residence until the mid 1850s when it became the Swan Hotel. In 1910 it changed its name to the Royal Hotel to avoid confusion with the Top Swan on the Lichfield Road.

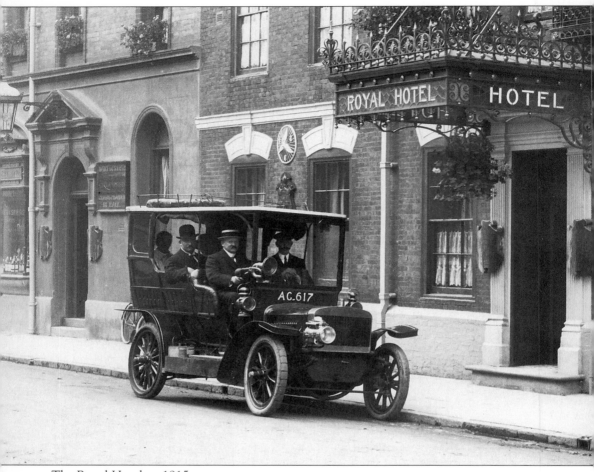

The Royal Hotel, *c.* 1915.

The Old Swan Hotel.

The old Sutton Coldfield Police Court in Station Street was used from about 1886 to 1960. It was demolished in 1967.

An early photograph of Sutton Station: the lack of refreshment rooms and the absence of the
Royal Hotel in the background indicate an early date — 1862 or 1863. The station opened on
2 June 1863.

Sutton Station, *c.* 1870, with the added refreshment rooms in the foreground. The wagon turntable and clock are shown. The line was extended from Sutton to Lichfield in 1884 opening for goods and passengers in December at a cost of around £90,000.

Sutton Town Station, Midland Railway (closed 1923), 1887. The Midland Railway provided access between Birmingham and Wolverhampton from 1872. It ceased as a passenger line in January 1965.

Royal Hotel, 1865. Originally opened as Sutton Coldfield's Royal Hotel in May 1865 it became a sanatorium in June 1896. In 1902 Sutton Council purchased the building for municipal offices and it was extended in 1906 to provide a Town Hall and fire station. An annex to the Town Hall was added in 1937.

The first Town Council and the first meeting of the Council, Sutton Coldfield, 1886.

All the Mayors of Sutton Coldfield from 1886-1911 outside the Council House in 1911.

Meeting of the British Association at Sutton Coldfield Town Hall, 1913.

The Council House, *c.* 1902.

Proclamation of George V, 1911. The Proclamation was read by the Mayor, T.H. Cartwright, from the balcony of the Town Hall to the people assembled in King Edward's Square.

A Royal Proclamation on the accession of Queen Elizabeth II, 1952.

Moat House, Lichfield Road.
Built by William Wilson *c.* 1680
for his own occupation on his
marriage to the widow Jane
Pudsey.

Ivy Cottages, Lichfield Road.
The cottages were demolished in
August 1963.

Cock Sparrow Hall, 1856, by Grundy. Cock Sparrow Hall, a half timbered black and white house, stood near to the Moat House. Its disappearance from the scene prompted Holbeche in his diary of *c.* 1892 to say, 'May the possessor of the property be forgiven for demolishing it, for it was wanton; a pure piece of vandalism'.

Opposite: Bishop Vesey Grammar School, 1887. The original school stood on Trinity Hill. The building on Lichfield Road was built in 1879 on land belonging to the Corporation of Sutton Coldfield.

Swan Inn and Grammar School, 1795. The old inn was known as the Top Swan to distinguish it from the hotel further down the High Street. It was mentioned in the year 1782 when Herr C.P. Mority, a German traveller, stayed overnight. For supper, bed and breakfast he was charged one shilling.

Sir William Anson opens new buildings at Bishop Vesey Grammar School, 1906.

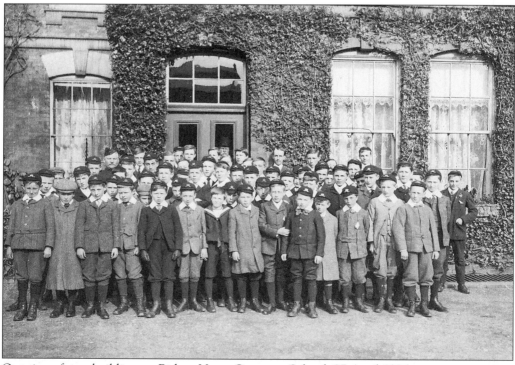

Opening of new buildings at Bishop Vesey Grammar School, 27 April 1906.

Five

Sutton Park

Park Road, built and paid for by Sir Edmund Hartop of Four Oaks Hall in 1826 to provide a direct approach to Sutton Park from the town.

Town Gate, Sutton Park. The original entrance to Sutton Park was at Wyndley Gate via Manor Hill. In 1826 Sir Edmund Hartop of Four Oaks Hall acquired sixty-three acres of the Park in Four Oaks in exchange for Meadow Platt. He then had Park Road cut which allowed the public access to Meadow Platt and the rest of Sutton Park.

The Crystal Palace fifteen inch gauge railway. The railway opened in June 1907 having been moved from Abingdon Park, Northampton. The line was approximately 1000 feet in length running from a point near Crystal Palace back towards the Wyndley Pool entrance gate. This is the ten and a quarter inch gauge railway. Nipper is the steam locomotive. The second and third passengers are Misses Townsend, whose family operated tea rooms in the park for many years.

Miniature railway at Crystal Palace. The Sutton Belle arrived at the Sutton site in 1948.

View showing Crystal Palace on the right, Holy Trinity Church in the centre, and Sutton's Town Hall on the left.

Crystal Palace. In 1868 Mr Joe Cole, a market gardener from Perry Barr, opened the Royal Promenade Gardens on a thirty-acre site between the town and the park. A major feature of the development was the crystal palace, a large conservatory accommodating up to two thousand people reminiscent of the famous Crystal Palace in Hyde Park, London.

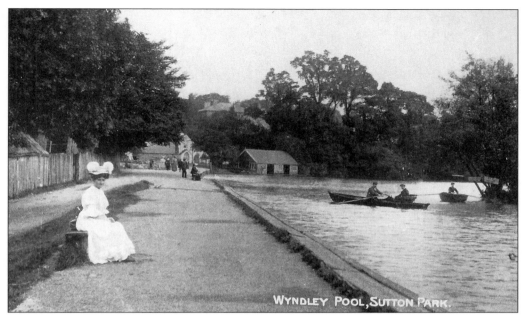

Wyndley Pool. During the reign of Henry V (1413-1422), five pools all with costly heads of stone were constructed. These were attributed to the Earl of Warwick. It is probable that Wyndley Pool was one of them. When John Leyland, the King's Antiquary, visited Sutton Coldfield in 1535 he recorded the existence of a pool called 'Wyndle'.

Wyndley Pool with the Water Mill on the right. A mill existed at Wyndley Pool from the seventeenth century onwards. Originally used as a blade mill, it was converted to a saw mill in 1840. The Mill was demolished in 1962-63.

Official opening of the Keepers Pool Swimming Baths on 30 July 1887.

Keepers Pool, 1888.

Keepers Pool and Baths. Keepers Pool, it is said, was constructed by John Holte, keeper of the Chase in Henry VI's time, hence the name Keepers Pool.

Fishing Party, *c.* 1887.

Longmoor Mill and Pool. Longmoor Pool was created in 1733 by John Riland. He applied to the Warden and Society for permission to build a dam across the valley at Longmoor. The stream ran unimpeded through the valley and there was no bridge to carry the traffic across. Once the dam was erected there was easier access to the Park. The corn mill was erected in 1754. It became button mill in 1762 and was demolished in 1938.

Powells Pool with the Old Slade Mill in the background. The steamboat Foam was first used in 1892. In 1730, Sir Thomas Holte erected a dam across the meadow below Stonehouse Farm to create a pool of thirty-five acres, the largest in the district, which twenty years later became known as Powells Pool after William Powell who worked a rolling mill there.

German prisoners of war near Longmoor Pool.

The Banners Gate entrance to Sutton Park.

Pentland Robins in Sutton Park, 1900.

Poor children of Birmingham in Sutton Park, 1898. Summer outings for the children were provided by the Birmingham Cinderella Club.

Rowton Well. Rowton Well's waters were famous for curing 'inveterate, cutaneous and chronic ailments' in 1762. In the last century the water was used by the Birmingham Eye Hospital to bathe patients' eyes.

Boldmere Gate. Bringing home the holly, December 1938. Holly was distributed in bundles to the residents of Sutton Coldfield for many years, but demand became so great that it was abandoned as being impractical in 1965.

Maypole dancing in Sutton Park in 1897, the Diamond Jubilee of Queen Victoria. The custom of maypole dancing was revived in Sutton by Benjamin Stone and on 29 November 1889, Benjamin Stone and four of the girl dancers went to Windsor Castle to present photographs of the maypole to the Queen.

Sutton Park Keeper, 1887.

Blackroot Pool. On 26 September 1757 'Mr Dolphin and Mr Homer shall have liberty to make a drain or pool in the valley below Black Root … to hold for 42 years at one shilling paid yearly … '

Blackroot Pool. It is believed the pool was given its name by the fact that the blackened root or stump of an oak tree stood on a mound near the centre of the pool.

Blackroot Pool and boathouse. In 1759 permission was given to Messrs Dolphin, Homer and Duncumb to erect a water wheel and building for a mill for dressing leather. Evidence is hard to come by that the leather mill was ever built, but the pool's water was used to work the sawmill situated in the gravel pit adjacent to the pool.

The 2nd City Battalion Royal Warwickshire Regiment, 1915. The regiment used Sutton Park as a training ground and camping site. The Headquarters was in huts near Powells Pool. In the photograph the soldiers are on Sutton Park Station.

The road from Blackroot to Common, 1887.

Queen Victoria's Golden Jubilee, Maypole Dancing, 1887.

Jubilee tree planting, 1887, to mark the Golden Jubilee of Queen Victoria.

Bracebridge Pool and boat house. Bracebridge Pool was formed around 1420 when the pool was leased to Sir Ralph Bracebridge at a yearly rent of either £10 or 120 bream.

Bracebridge Cottage and Pool, 1895. in 1921 a catering business was started at Bracebridge Cottage. In 1981, Mr C. Barsby and his wife Celia ran the cottage as a restaurant for twelve months. In 1983 the restaurant opened as Bobby Browns.

Druids Well, 1910. In 1813, Sutton Coldfield Corporation proposed that the pits and springs in Sutton Park should be put to public use. In 1815, wells were made on the springs at Pool Hollies Wood (Druids Well) and at Keepers Pool. Vandals reduced Druids Well to a pile of rubble in 1982.

The Gumslade, Sutton Park. In Old English, 'slade' means 'valley', in this case relating to the broad, low lying path through the Gum Slade. The lovely glade is overhung with massive ancient oaks over 250 years old, and skirted on each side with shelving banks full of cosy nooks and natural arbours.

One of the ancient oaks in the Gumslade. Some of the oldest trees in the Park can be found in this area.

The Four Oaks entrance to Sutton Park, *c.* 1905.

Children's boating pool, Blackroot Pool.

Children's paddling steamer, Plantsbrook Stream, near Keepers Pool.

Six
Four Oaks and Mere Green

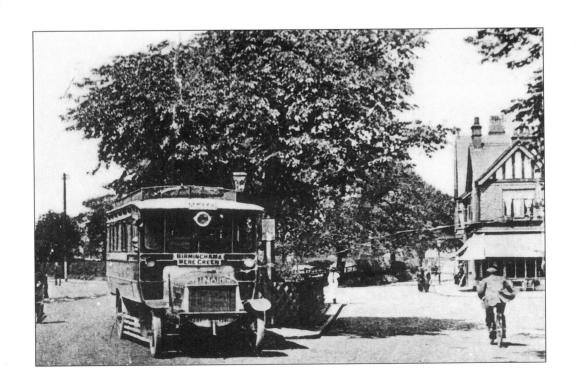

Four Oaks Hall, built by Henry, third Lord Ffolliot of Ballyshannon at the end of the seventeenth century. The architect was William Wilson. It is believed Sir William Hartopp entertained King Edward VII here in 1901. The house was demolished sometime prior to 1908.

The Great Hall, Four Oaks, 1895.

The Hartopp family sold the Four Oaks Estate comprising some 246 acres for £60,000 to a racecourse company in the 1870s. In 1879, the course opened with a National Hunt Steeplechase. Sadly the course failed and in 1890 the course with all its equipment was auctioned off.

The Royal Agricultural Show, Four Oaks, June 1898. The show, situated in the grounds of Four Oaks Hall, was attended by Edward VII when he was Prince of Wales.

Construction work at Four Oaks Station, *c.* 1887. Four Oaks Station was opened by the London and North Western on 15 December 1884.

Mere Green, *c.* 1920. The Chester Road to Mere Green service, which called at Sutton Coldfield, was the first bus route in the area.

Mere Green Road looking towards the Barley Mow public house, 1908. The advertising placard on the right reads 'blacking, lace and boot dressings of all kinds kept in stock'.

View of Four Oaks from Four Oaks Tower, *c.* 1900.

Four Oaks Tower, Hill Village Road, *c.* 1900. The eighty-foot-high red brick tower was built between 1892 and 1895, to the requirements of the eccentric retired pawn broker from Tipton, Hugh Lewis. Known locally as 'Lewis's Folly', it was demolished just before the First World War.

Number 82-88 Hill Village Road, corner of Hill Village Road and Sherifoot Lane. The end building was formerly a slaughterhouse and was demolished in May 1956.

Hill Village Road, numbers 82, 94, 86, and 88.

The White Lion, *c.* 1900, Hill Village Road. The old buildings were demolished in 1969, the new pub being situated at the rear of the then existing premises, which were more than 150 years old.

Hill Village Road. Old Cottage opposite the White Lion Inn, demolished in 1960. Locals maintain it was originally the Lamb Public House, but no evidence to support this claim has yet been found.

Moor Hall Farmhouse. This fifteenth-century sandstone building is believed to have been built by William Harman, father of John Harman (Bishop Vesey), who became Sutton's greatest benefactor.

Little Sutton and Moor Hall

Moor Hall Farmhouse. This fifteenth-century sandstone building is believed to have been built by William Harman, father of John Harman (Bishop Vesey).

Moor Hall Farmhouse

Moor Hall, built for Bishop Vesey, *c.* 1527 after he had obtained certain lands called Moor Crofts and Heath Yards with permission to enclose forty acres of waste land, at a cost of £1,500. The Bishop employed a retinue of 140 men which he required to be dressed in scarlet caps and gowns.

Moor Hall was greatly added to in the eighteenth century.

The demolition of Moor Hall in 1904 after its acquisition by Alderman Edward Ansall of Rigby Hall, Bromsgrove. The house had been rebuilt three or four times since Bishop Vesey had it built. The present-day building is a hotel.

The summer of 1904, and these three children, protected from the sun by their bonnets, stand with their father in front of the remains of Moor Hall.

Moor Hall, 1907. The present Moor Hall was erected in 1905 when the Hall was the private residence of Colonel Ansell of the Birmingham brewery company. In 1930 the Moor Hall Park including all the parklands, farmhouses and lodges were put up for sale at an auction in Birmingham. The highest bidder was Mr W. Streather, founder of a local building company. Mr Streather immediatly converted the Hall into a private hotel, had part of the grounds laid out as a golf course and built a clubhouse for the golfers. This is the present Moor Hall Golf Club.

Moor Hall, 1907.

The Cockpit at Moor Hall, 1907. A local historian says that in the woods near Moor Hall there was a large bear pit with walls of old sandstone, which was later made into an ornamental water garden with embellishments in different kinds of stone. Could it be that the Cock Pit and bear pit were one and the same place?

Moor Hall. The Ansell family, 1907.

The gates of Ashfurlong Hall, which were sold to prevent them going for scrap during the Second World War. The lady in the photograph is Lil Grundy.

Ashfurlong Hall, c. 1907. The old part of Ashfurlong Hall is an example of a massive farm building incorporating a small early sixteenth century house of a similar style to the Vesey cottages. The present house was rebuilt by Mr Vaughton, who was High Sheriff of Warwickshire in 1804.

Ashfurlong Hall.

Opposite: Standing on Little Sutton Lane, this Bishop Vesey Cottage was demolished in 1959.

Ashfurlong Hall. The Wilkinson family, 1907.

Little Sutton Baptist Chapel, Slade Road. Little Sutton Baptist Church as shown in this photograph was built and opened in April 1869. It was built on the site of an earlier chapel of 1774. Standing in Slade Road, the chapel was used until the new building in Grange Road was erected.

Little Sutton Baptist Chapel. Sunday School congregation, *c.* 1925.

Reddicap and
Whitehouse Common

Vesey Cottage, High Heath, 1887. The smallest of the Vesey Cottages, it measures twenty-one feet six inches by eighteen feet, and there is only one room on each floor. It stands near the footpath between Tamworth Road and Withy Hill Road.

White House Farm stood at the junction of Rectory Road and Hollyfield Road and is seen here in June 1950.

Jame's Pool, 1950, which used to be situated between Whitehouse Common Road and Bedford Road, just off Barnard Road.

The Grounds to The Rectory. In 1940 the Sutton Coldfield Corporation purchased the 74 acres 18 perchases for £16,250 from the Ecclesiastical commisioners and the area became Rectory Park.

Sutton Coldfield Rectory, the home of the Revd W.K. Riland Bedford, rector of Sutton Coldfield from 1850 to 1892. In 1701, John Riland was determined to erect a rectory house in the fields opposite to the old glebe; he contracted with his builder for a house forty-five feet long in front and thirty-five feet deep and twenty-three feet high to the wall plate, for the sum of £239 11s 3d. It was demolished in 1936.

The Rectory.

The Free Foresters, Rectory Park. The Free Foresters Cricket Club was founded by the Revd W.K. Riland Bedford, and they used to play here at Rectory Park. The Club included some of the leading cricketers in England. Riland Bedford and W.E.W. Collins wrote a history of the club called *Annals of the Free Foresters 1856-1894* in 1895.

A Vesey House near the Rectory. This cottage is a good example of a building designed to house the weaving trade known as kersey, which was introduced into Sutton Coldfield by Bishop Vesey in Tudor times.

The Mount, Reddicap Hill. The Mount was built for John Lilly probably some time in the 1870s. By 1965 the house had been demolished and in 1967 the official opening of the Council-built flats and maisonettes took place.

Reddicap Hill.

Reddicap Hill.

Nine
Walmley

Penns Lane, *c*. 1890. Bridge over Plantsbrook stream.

Penns Station, opened on the Midland line in 1879. It was closed as a passenger line in 1965, the last station master being Mr Les Hollins.

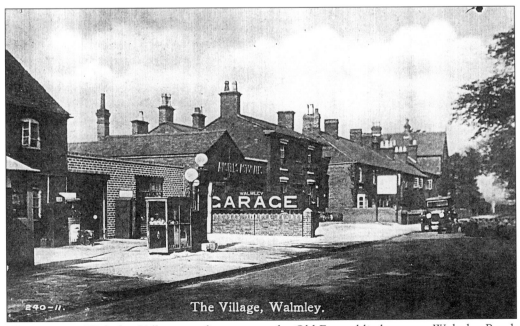

The garage in Walmley Village standing next to the Old Fox public house on Walmley Road. The garage was next to the Post Office and just across the road from the cottages shown in the background were the shops, c. 1930.

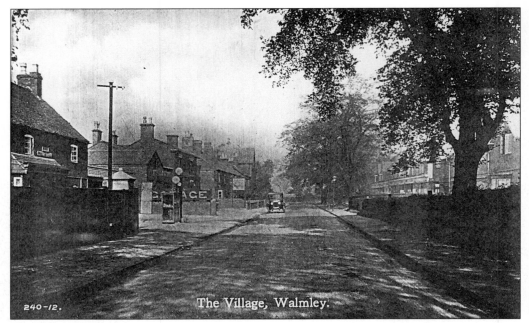

The Village, Walmley.

Walmley Post Office and General Stores, which stood in Walmley Road near Walmley Close. It was demolished c. 1959.

144

St. John's Church, Walmley, built of Staffordshire blue brick was consecrated on 2nd September 1845. It was paid for by a donation of £1,000 from Miss Lucy Riland, a relative of the Revd W.R. Bedford, and £4,000 raised by subscriptions together with the proceeds of a bazaar held in Sutton Park. The land was given by Sutton Coldfield Corporation.

Walmley War Memorial and Alms Houses. The War memorial was erected by public subscription and unveiled in December 1920. The Alms Houses behind the war memorial were built in 1863.

In 1825 it was decided to build ten almshouses throughout Sutton Coldfield for the poor inhabitants. They consisted of two ground floor rooms with a cellar and were inhabited by ten poor persons or old men and their wives. The almshouses in Walmley in Fox Hollies Road appear to have been built in 1828. This photo shows the later almhouses built in 1863. These stand in front of the 1828 almhouses.

146

Vesey House, Newhall Lane, now Wylde Green Road, 1892. Known as Ford Keepers Cottage, the cottage was built by Plantsbrook stream. The keeper at the cottage would help to guide people across the stream as there was no bridge. This road used to be the main route to Coleshill.

New Hall Mill, 1907. New Hall Mill is Sutton Coldfield's only complete working mill. Probably built between 1582 and 1638, it is constructed of local red brick. The three-storey watermill stands next to the mill pool which is fed from Plantsbrook stream. The mill is used for grinding corn.

New Hall Mill, 1907.

Wincelle, a sixteenth-century timber-framed house, which was moved from its original site on Wiggins Hill and installed in Wylde Green Road in 1910. The work was to the order of Mr Walter Wilkinson, who owned the nearby New Hall. With the infilling removed ready for its move it was photographed by Sir Benjamin Stone in 1910.

New Hall, 1907. The first written mention of New Hall dates from 1341, but it is believed to date from *c.* 1200. As Sutton Coldfield's Grade 1 listed building, today it is a luxury hotel.

A Vesey Club visit to New Hall in 1908. The house is completely moated, the moat being fed from seven nearby springs.

New Hall. Interior view of the Great Chamber built in the 1500s. This photograph was taken in about 1925.

The Vesey Club at New Hall in 1908. The Vesey Club was formed as a literary and scientific association at a meeting at the Town Hall on 30 July 1988. Sir Benjamin Stone was its first president.

Four generations of the Healey Family at New hall in 1895, who were the owners of the Hall when it was a boys' college from 1885 to 1903.

New Hall Boys' School, 1892. The College was opened in 1885 with Mr F.W.W. Howell as principal. In 1891 with the death of Mr Howell, the college was run by Mr J. Everard Healey and his son.

New Hall Chapel. Built in the seventeenth century, this building has been used as a stable, a carpenter's shop, and a gymnasium. It is believed it was built by Henry Sacheverell, and its size of windows suggests that it was originally used as a chapel.

Opposite: School boys at New Hall, 1895. Pupils were prepared for either professional or commercial careers. The place must have been remarkably healthy, for no illness was recorded for three years. Nonetheless the school presumably failed to succeed for in 1903 New Hall was purchased by Walter Wilkinson.

Often attributed to Sir Williamson Wilson, this was the stable block to Langley Hall. The sixteenth-century stables became a farmhouse and after an uncertain future in the 1980s, this Grade 2 listed building was converted into twelve luxury town houses in the late 1980s.

The bridge over the moat at Peddimore Hall, 1890.

Peddimore Hall, 1892, with Mr and Mrs King, his sister and children.

Opposite: The Plough Inn, Minworth. The Inn was listed in the 1924 *Directory*, but it had gone by the time the 1932 *Directory* was published.

Peddimore Hall. The present hall, now a farmhouse in Peddimore Lane, Walmley, stands on the site of a much earlier hall dating back to 1281. Once owned by the Arden family, the present building dates back to 1659. It is unusual in that it is surrounded by a double moat.

A pre-1936 boundary sign of Sutton Coldfield at Watford Gap.

IMAGES
of England

SUTTON COLDFIELD
THE SECOND SELECTION

Compiled by
Marian Baxter

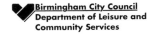
Birmingham City Council
Department of Leisure and
Community Services

TEMPUS

Contents

Acknowledgements

My thanks go to Birmingham City Council, Department of Leisure and Community Services, Libraries and Learning, for allowing me to use their photographs.

Thanks to Martin Flynn, Central Library Manager, Birmingham Central Library and David Buxton of Chalford Publishing Co. who, after the success of the first volume, encouraged me to put together this second volume. Thanks also to several individuals who have given valuable information and, or, lent me material for inclusion in this book. Thanks to Roger Lea and Robert Pritchard for the use of their photographs. Special thanks to John McCormack who has carried out several comprehensive photographic surveys of recent development sites in Sutton Coldfield over the last five years.

Particular thanks to Geoff Cashmore who has done all the proof reading and, yet again, sorted out the computer every time the computer illiterate author pressed the wrong buttons.

Introduction

After the huge success of the first collection of photographs relating to Sutton Coldfield, I felt there were still many more images of the area, something near 6,000 are housed in the Sutton Coldfield Local Studies Department of the Sutton Coldfield Central Library, which warranted producing a second volume. The first collection covered the Sutton area from the 1800s to the turn of the century and beyond to the 1930s. With the ever-increasing and on-going development of any area, Sutton Coldfield is no exception to change, and this volume brings Sutton up to the end of 1995. The aim is to show how much has survived and how much has been lost. Most of the photographs included here are of historic and nostalgic content. They are a record of many of the events and issues which have evoked public interest, concern, sympathy and other mixed emotions over the past century.

Today Sutton Coldfield is made up of three wards, Four Oaks, New Hall and Vesey, making it the largest constituency in Birmingham, covering just over one fifth of Birmingham's administrative area. It is the most northerly constituency and borders the Staffordshire and Warwickshire countryside. The suburban area is characterised by a predominance of pre- and post-war owner occupied housing, the majority of it built in an *ad hoc* pattern. Moreover, its growth as a suburban town has been accompanied by virtually no large scale industrial development. In fact, where areas have been developed, it has been confined to light and service industries. Sutton Coldfield is not unlike many of Britain's towns in terms of its character and nature of development. However, it differs from the majority of Birmingham's other suburbs in that its development does reflect the combination of low density housing and the large land area of the constituency. Sutton Coldfield accounts for twenty per cent of Birmingham's land area, but contains only ten per cent of its population.

The Four Oaks Ward is the most northern ward of the city. It is characterised by the attractive, well established residential areas of Four Oaks, Little Sutton, Reddicap Heath and Mere Green, and by the extensive areas of open space at Sutton Park and Rectory Park, as well as large areas of Green Belt land to the east. The New Hall Ward lies in the north east corner of the city and contains the communities of Falcon Lodge, Minworth, Reddicap Heath, Walmley and part of Whitehouse Common. Sutton Town Centre also lies within this ward. New Hall is an unusual ward within Birmingham in that it includes significant areas of open countryside; it is also the largest ward within the city in terms of area. The 1991 Census showed that the residential population was 31,051, an increase of over twelve per cent on the 1981 figure. This is by far the largest rate of growth in Birmingham and reflects the fact that the New Hall Ward has witnessed a significant growth in its housing area in recent years. The Vesey Ward lies to the south of the Sutton Town Centre and includes Boldmere, parts of New Oscott and Walmley, Wylde Green and part of Sutton Park.

Like any large area, there are many issues which have fuelled fires of discontent over the ensuing years, including the loss of local government facilities and the closure of the council offices, massive overspill building programmes on its Green Belt land and more recently, the approval of the building of the Birmingham Northern Relief Road, Britain's first toll road, as well as the large business park development at Peddimore in Walmley. However, no town stands still. Sutton Town Centre has grown rapidly since the 1960s; with the newly completed New Hall Walk shopping centre just finished in 1997, Sutton is now the second largest shopping centre in Birmingham. With the 2,400 acres of Sutton Park receiving the status of a National Nature Reserve and the New Valley Country Park plans well on the way to completion, Sutton Coldfield has a challenging and exciting future to look forward to.

One
Wylde Green

Birmingham Road, Wylde Green, *c.* 1988.

Chester Road and Birmingham Road junction on the border of Birmingham and Sutton
Coldfield, April 1939.

Birmingham Road, c. 1988. 'Books old and new' was an appropriate sign for what was Bracken
Books. Named after Miss Bracken, who wrote a history of Sutton Coldfield, the book shop was
run by Mr William Gavin for over fifty years. He was also a craftsman in wood. The limited
space in the 250 year old converted cottage was used to great advantage. The cottages were
demolished in 1988 and replaced by modern buildings.

Ansey Physical Training College. Miss Rhoda Ansey purchased what was Yew Tree House on the Chester Road in 1907. Fees at the college, which specialised in women's physical training, were 35 guineas per term. Students were admitted between the ages of 18 and 28.

The Quadrangle. Fees covered tuition, public examinations, travelling expenses in connection with university lectures, hockey, lacrosse and netball matches played by the college, medical examinations at the beginning and end of the course, board residence and plain laundry. The regulation costume, games equipment and books were not included.

Remedial treatment. The college celebrated its 75th anniversary in 1972. It had grown from three private, paying students to 192 grant aided students and eight in-service teachers; from a two year training to a four year training; from the theory and practice of Swedish Educational and Medical Gymnastics to a BEd degree. However it was not to survive, and the college closed in the late 1970s.

The study bedroom.

Cottages on Gravelly Lane, the site of the Wylde Green Pavilion Cinema. The Pavilion, built on the site of the old cottages, was designed by Harold Seymore Scout and built by G.T. Stephens and Son. It opened on 10 October 1931 with a showing of the *British Movietone News*, *Our Nagging Wives*, (a comedy) and *The Sport of Kings* starring Leslie Henson, Dorothy Boyd and Gordon Harker, plus an organ recital by Frank Matthews on the 3c/9 Christie organ, the first to be installed in a Birmingham cinema. Despite making a profit, The Pavilion was chosen as the venue for the first ten pin bowling alley in the Midlands and the cinema was converted. However the craze was short lived and the ABC Bowl as it was known, was demolished in 1974.

The Pavilion Cinema, 1938.

Marchmont House. This was built on the Birmingham Road in 1853 for Henry Fielding, a silverware manufacturer from Birmingham. The house was situated in large, laid out grounds. It was approached by a winding drive through a substantial garden with croquet lawns, shrubberies and trees. To the side of the house were the stables, carriage house, gardener's and groom's cottages. Behind there was a pleasure garden, a large area of lawns and paths and beyond this, the paddock for the horses.

The croquet lawn at Marchmont House. The boundary paddock finished approximately where Brooks Road, near Walmley Golf Course, is situated today. In the 1950s the large old houses in that area were demolished and the Woodlands Estate was built, covering the present day thoroughfares of Marchmont Road, Hillcrest Road, Woodleigh Road, Britton Drive, Hilton Drive, Simpson Road and parts of Oakhurst Road and Hawthorne Road. All that remains of the Victorian houses are their names incorporated in road names, a few old trees and the remains of garden walls on the present estate.

Birmingham Road, Wylde Green, near the corner of Vesey Road. The painted pedestrian crossing is being installed in 1938.

The shop of Charles Nuttall, trade name T. Voice, in Station Road, 1938.

Wylde Green station, date unknown. The station was opened on 2 June 1862 and it was the last station before Sutton Coldfield until the line was extended to Lichfield in 1884.

Two

Boldmere

Flooding under the railway bridge at Chester Road, 8 August 1948.

Highbridge Road shops, April 1937.

A new drain cleaning vehicle on Highbridge Road, January 1938.

Air raid damage to a 12 inch water main, Jockey Road, 17 May 1941. Approximately seventy to eighty bombs fell on Sutton Coldfield during the Second World War.

Jockey Road.

The Gate Inn, Boldmere Road, with the adjacent cottages being prepared for demolition in 1938. They were replaced by the Boldmere public house.

Boldmere Road and the corner of Antrobus Road and Highbridge Road.

Three
Maney

Birmingham Road from The Cup, 1887.

The Horse and Jockey Inn at the turn of the century, on the corner of Jockey Road. The landlord was T.W. Wilson in 1900.

Maney Iron Church, *c*. 1880, drawn by K.J. Williams. The Iron Church, so called because it was built of corrugated iron, stood by the Smithy. It was built in 1877 and was used until 1904 when the foundation stone was laid for St Peter's. An article in *The Sutton Coldfield News* of 1878 describes the church as 'clean and commodious, but its low roof is oppressive and gives the building a somewhat shed-like appearance. There was a great deal of colour in the building, which gave the impression to the visitor of being stagey.'

The Stone House, 1988. This is the largest of the fifty-one stone houses reputably built by Bishop Vesey. The large window on the ground floor indicates that the cottage was used for the local weaving industry known as 'kersey', introduced into the area by the bishop. Built of local sandstone, the cottage measures 33 ft long and 20 ft wide.

Interior of The Stone House, 1940.

A wedding group at Clovelly House, which stood opposite Shakespeare House on the Birmingham Road, which can just be seen in the background to the left.

Maney Bridge.

Interior of Maney Hall. The hall belonged to St Peter's Church and stood on the corners of Birmingham Road and Maney Hill Road. An article from the local newspaper of the time, *The Sutton Coldfield News* of 1982, quotes, 'The Maney Christmas Party has, since its inception twelve years ago, become increasingly popular, and is now an important event in the social programme associated with St Peter's Church. Although the attendance at this year's party held on Friday at St Peter's was adversely affected by influenza, the gathering was an exceedingly happy one.' The site is now occupied by flats.

The Smithy. Adjoining Bodington Gardens, this fourteenth century building was once the home of the blacksmith, whose forge originally stood at the corner of Church Road and Maney Road. For a time it was museum. Today called The Driffold Gallery, it sells nineteenth and twentieth century paintings. Inspection at the rear reveals its cruck frame, confirming this as one of Sutton Coldfield's oldest buildings.

The rear of The Smithy, showing the cruck beam.

Birmingham Road, 1939, looking to Maney Corner. The Smithy can be seen on the left side of the road. The hedge by The Smithy borders the grounds of what is now Bodington Gardens. The cottages behind The Smithy are on Church Road.

Maney Corner, 1939; Birmingham Road at the corners of Maney Hill Road and Church Road.

Yew Tree Cottages on The Driffold, 1958. On the back of the photograph these cottages are called 'Wren's Nest House'. The 1958 directory of Sutton Coldfield lists six residents at Yew Tree Cottages. The 1960 directory does not have an entry for them so presumably they had been demolished. But why Wren's Nest House? The author would be interested to hear from anyone who could answer this question.

The White House. Dr Bodington's surgery in Maney, called the White House, stood on the site of the Odeon Cinema. In the mid 1800s Dr Bodington successfully treated people suffering from pulmonia tuberculosis using his pioneering open air treatment, until the arrival of modern drugs. He saved many thousands of lives, for which he gained national acclaim.

The rear of Bragg's Farm. Opposite the Odeon Cinema stands Vesey Manor, a sandstone building which today sells antiques. In the early part of the century it was known as Bragg's Farm.

Drawing of Bragg's Farm.

Sutton Coldfield in 1863, as viewed by Miss Agnes Bracken. The horse and cart are standing outside The Cup Inn. The building with the three chimneys in the centre is The Old Pie Shop. The open space to the left of The Old Pie Shop is where Gracechurch Shopping Centre stands today and the buildings above that are those on Mill Street.

The Cup Inn. This was, and is, an attractive wayside inn situated at Maney on the main road between Lichfield and Birmingham. Being at the bottom of Maney Hill it was not far from the Wyndley Pool entrance to Sutton Park and must have enjoyed considerable custom from passing trade. It catered for visitors to Sutton, offering first class accommodation for their horses and carriages. Mary Ellery was its proprietress in the 1800s and she was able to offer chops, steaks and teas at three minutes notice. During the summer dancing was held on the lawn behind.

30

The Cup on the Birmingham Road, *c.* 1968. The old, single storey, wayside inn was demolished in 1893 and by November 1894, a much larger and more modern Cup was erected in its place.

Holland House from the road. It is difficult to associate Sutton Coldfield with the manufacture of guns, but such was the diversity of trade carried out by the various water mills in Sutton that one of them in the eighteenth century could be found actively employed making gun barrels and bayonets. The mill was situated in Holland Road, where Plantsbrook School now stands.

Gardens at the rear of Holland House. Built in 1732, the *Holbeche Diary* of 1892 describes the house in 1855 as follows: 'Mrs Oughton lived at Holland House which was unlike what it is now. Several pools surrounded by evergreens took up what is now the garden. There was a long porch in front of the house with a trellis work side... it was very deep and had white steps and a pavement.'

The gardens at the rear. 'Beyond there were three pools and a mill dam, on which a mill in which bayonets and gun barrels were found. Another dam which divided the ozier beds (willow beds) has been removed.' The date when the mill ceased work is not known, but it had probably finished working by 1889. In 1933 the reed beds still existed in the area, but the pool had been filled in. Holland House was demolished in 1936, the mill having gone long before. Finally, in 1939, on the site once occupied by Holland House, Riland Bedford Secondary School, renamed Plantsbrook School in 1986, was built.

Four

Four Oaks and
Mere Green

Hill Hook Pool, 1982.

Lichfield Road, with Little Sutton Lane on the right and Barker Road on the left, c. 1930.

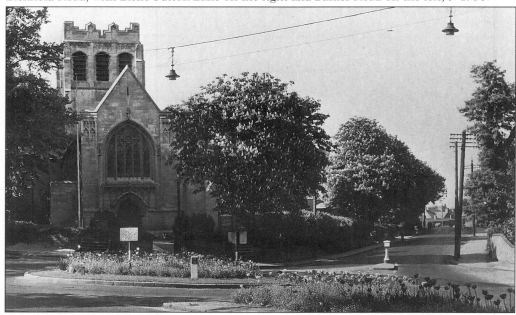

Lichfield Road and Four Oaks Methodist Church, June 1951. The scheme for the erection of a Wesleyan Church at Four Oaks was initiated on 8 February 1902 and within a month nearly £1,300 was promised. Plans were prepared by Messrs Crouch, Butler and Savage of Birmingham, for the erection of the complete church, schools and caretaker's house at an established cost between £10,000 and £11,000, exclusive of land. The stone-laying ceremony took place on 22 October 1902 and on 3 October 1903, the opening services were held.

Four Oaks Road, date unknown, showing three of the four oaks from which it is believed Four Oaks got its name. The four trees are shown on a map of 1811; one was cut down due to disease. The trees stand on the corner of Hartop Road and Four Oaks Road.

Burcote Grange High School for Girls, from Four Oaks Road. The boarding and day school for girls between the ages of 4 to 14 opened in 1910. A leaflet of 1914 tells us that the principals were Mrs Preston and Miss Ethel Rowe, assisted by the French and German governesses and by an efficient staff of fully qualified teachers.

Burcote Grange High School, classroom. The fees at that time were fifteen guineas a term for weekly boarders and twenty guineas for full boarders.

Burcote Grange School, dining room. The private school closed in July 1989 due to 'escalating costs'.

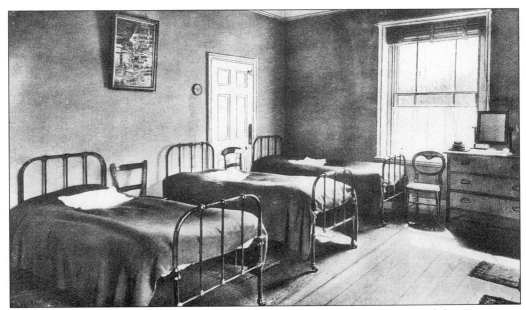

Burcote Grange School, dormitory. The school has now been transformed by Bovis into retirement homes which opened in 1995.

Four Oaks Road from Walsall Road.

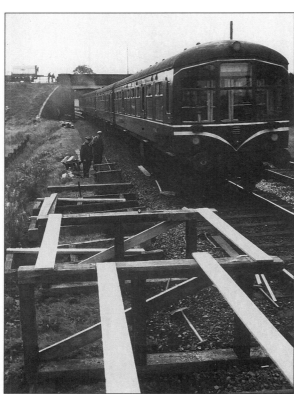

Butlers Lane Halt under construction, date unknown.

Blake Street station, November 1974.

On Stone by H.Harris

Printed by J.Walker

THIS VIEW OF ST. JAMES'S CHAPEL MEREGREEN

in the parish of Sutton Coldfield, is respectfully dedicated to the Hon. & Right Rev Henry Ryder
Lord Bishop of Lichfield & Coventry, & to the Rev. William Riland Bedford Rector of Sutton Coldfield,
by their Obedient Servant,
D.R. Hill
Architect

St James' Church, Hill, 1935. The church was consecrated in 1835 by Bishop Ryder, Bishop of Lichfield, building having started in 1834 on an economical structure of brick and plaster to seat about 300 people. In 1906 plans were put forward to rebuild the church. Mr Bateman, a local architect, put forward his plans in May 1907. The church has been refurbished for its 150th anniversary in 1997.

Was Mere Green named after the 'Mere', the pool which was situated on the triangular section near to Hill Village Road, Mere Green Road and Lichfield Road? Shown on an 1811 map the 'Mere' has gone by the time of the 25 inch first edition Ordnance Survey map.

Mere Green School. Whilst Town School in the centre of Sutton Coldfield was being established, one of the town's Corporation asked, in 1822, if the Warden and Society owned any suitable land in Hill for a school. It was agreed on 28 December 1822 'that a piece of land at Mere Pool, part of the waste containing more than a road, situate between Mere Green and Little Sutton be the place recommended for building the proposed Charity School.' In 1825 the school for twenty-five boys and twenty-five girls was established with the mistress being paid £30 per annum. The first master and mistress, Mr and Mrs Daniel Aulton, received a salary of £60 per term. The school still stands, although no longer used as such. A plaque on the wall reads 'Corporation School erected A.D. 1826'.

Houses on Mere Green Road.

SUTTON'S SMALLEST HOUSE
HILL VILLAGE ROAD
ONE UP ONE DOWN
HEIGHT TO EVES 14 FEET 2 INCHES
WIDTH 10 FEET 4 INCHES
~ DEMOLISHED JULY 1958.

B Williams
1990

Sutton Coldfield's smallest house, which stood on Hill Village Road, measured 14 ft 2 ins high and 10 ft 4 ins wide. It was demolished in July 1958.

Hill Village Road at the corner of Butlers Lane. The cottages on the corner were demolished in about 1960.

Hill Village Road.

The Old Farm House, 48 Hill Village Road.

The Malt House, number 27 Hill Village Road.

Hill Hook Mill, 1964. A water mill stood near the pool at Hill Hook for over 300 years. Unlike most of Sutton Coldfield's mills which were powered by the waters of Plantsbrook, Hill Hook had its own independent water supply in the form of a stream which flows north to Shenstone. The first known record of the mill is in 1671 when Oliver Cartwright was described as the 'Milleur at Hill'.

The site of Hill Hook Mill, 1962. The last occupier of the mill, Mr Medlam, was forced to leave due to ill health. After his departure the mill was vandalised, which led to its demolition.

The site of the water wheel, 1982. By 1979 the dam to the pool was in a badly neglected state, so the pool was emptied. The empty pool revealed the original gravel dam. The only part visible of the water wheel was the top part which had been broken by vandals.

Excavated site of the mill, 1983. In 1982 Birmingham City Council put forward £60,000 to repair and desilt the mill pool. At the same time the mill site was excavated, the wheel removed, restored and installed at Forge Mill, in Sandwell Valley.

The restored dam and new bridge, 1984. By March 1984 repairs had been completed, the pool refilled and the cellars of mill were filled in.

Five
Falcon Lodge and Whitehouse Common

The corner of Whitehouse Common and Tamworth Road, May 1962.

FRONT ELEVATION.

Falcon Lodge. A Georgian house, believed to have been built around 1820, is named Falcon Lodge in a lease of 1824 and the present day estate took its name from this house. The lease of 1824 to Mr William Pepper mentions the lodge with barn, stable, cow house, yard, garden and orchard. When put up for sale in August 1852, the sales catalogue describes the house as standing in 54 acres of superior meadow, pasture and arable land. The house contained a large entrance hall, dining and drawing rooms, nine bedrooms, store room and closets, a large kitchen, brewhouse and scullery, dairy, excellent cellars and other domestic conveniences.

Opposite: Fowler Road, 1950. In October 1948, the Borough Council agreed on the road names for the estate and in January 1949 the Mayor, Councillor C.H. Dainty, opened the first house on the estate. The 1959 *Sutton Coldfield Town Guide* describes the almost complete estate as 'a fine model estate comprising of some 1,539 houses attractively laid out, having an up to date shopping centre, and a community hall with a branch library.' The estate was considered to be well in advance of its time in layout and design.

Church Road, 1950. The estate was sold by Mr Cattell to the Corporation of Sutton Coldfield on 31 May 1937 for £39,500. The Corporation's intention to develop it as a housing estate was thwarted first by the war and then by government restrictions. In 1947 the Ministry of Works approved the Borough Surveyor's plans for roads and sewers and on 19 November, tenders were invited for the erection of twenty-eight houses on Springfield Road.

White House Farm, June 1950. The farm stood at the crossroads of Whitehouse Common Road and Rectory Road.

The Old Mission Room on Lindridge Road, July 1958.

Air raid damage on Whitehouse
Common Road, 27 August 1940.

Numbers 206-210 Whitehouse Common Road, 1971. These cottages used to stand on the corner of Whitehouse Road and Lindridge Road.

The corner of Whitehouse Common Road and the Tamworth Road, May 1962. This is now the site of the new health centre.

Rear view of the cottages at the corner of Whitehouse Common Road and Tamworth Road, May 1962.

One of the fifty-one Bishop Vesey cottages. This one stood on the corner of Whitehouse Common Road and Tamworth Road.

The White House, not to be confused with the White House which stood near Rectory Road, was demolished in December 1962.

The smallest of the Bishop Vesey cottages that survives stands at High Heath on the footpath between Tamworth Road and Withy Hill Road. It measures 21 ft 6 ins by 18 ft and there is only a single room on each floor. An unusual feature for cottages of the Tudor times was that the bedrooms on the first and second floors had fireplaces.

Six
Reddicap and Walmley

Widening the Eachlehurst Road near the Sutton Coldfield boundary, May 1938.

The Mount. 'A freehold house of outstanding character set in more than four acres of land' is how an estate agent's sales catalogue describes The Mount. Built in the late 1800s, possibly around 1879, it is described as 'A charming Victorian Residence suitable for a large family... Having the benefit on the ground floor of lounge, dining room, conservatory, Chinese room, breakfast room, kitchen, 'butlers pantry'... on the first floor master bedroom with superb *en suite* bathroom, five further bedrooms, large bathroom... tennis courts, summer house, stabling and pigsty.'

The new housing development The Mount, opened by the Duchess of Kent on 24 October 1967. The house was demolished in the early 1960s and tenders were invited for the new housing area. George Stubbings prepared Bills of Qualities in 1965. The accepted tender to the amount of £414,801,00 included one block of three storey maisonettes, (14 dwellings) one block of four storey maisonettes, (14 dwellings) two blocks of nine storey flats (each of 51 dwellings) fifty garages and a children's adventure playground.

Penns Hall. The Webster family are first recorded at Penns Mill in 1752, although it is believed they had been in possession of the site two years previously. Joseph Webster I moved to the house following his second marriage to Anne, the daughter of John Brodridd of Worcester in 1759. The first document relating to Penns is dated 1618, when the place was occupied by John Penn, hence the name Penns Hall. In 1855 James Horsfall joined forces with the Websters and in 1859 the mills were closed and the business transfered to Hay Mills. The hall was purchased by James Horsfall in 1865. In 1947 the property was purchased by Ansells and after alterations, the Penns Hall Hotel opened in 1950.

Penns Lane Cottages. With the expanding business at Penns Mill, Joseph Webster III needed housing for his increasing workforce. He decided to build the houses on his land near Walmley and the cottages were built in 1812. There were similar cottages some 30 yards north which were demolished when the railway was built. The cottages were demolished in 1984 despite efforts by the local residents to save them. Today the flats of Arbour Court stand on the site.

The almshouses in Walmley. In 1826 it was decided to build ten almshouses throughout Sutton for the poor inhabitants. These consisted of two ground floor rooms with a cellar and were inhabited by ten poor persons or old men and their wives. The almshouses in Walmley were built in Fox Hollies Road in 1828.

Princess Anne is greeted by the Worshipful Mayor of Sutton Coldfield, Alderman Mrs E.E. Dunnett at the opening of Lingard House in 1971.

Her Royal Highness meets the residents. A further five almshouses were built in 1863 on the corner of Fox Hollies Road and Walmley Road and further buildings constructed in 1971 were given the name Lingard House. Owned by the Sutton Coldfield Municipal Charities they still offer accommodation to the older inhabitants of Sutton Coldfield.

The Princess talks to local school children during her visit.

St John's Church, Walmley, 1982. Walmley was just a quiet village with scattered farms when St John's was built in 1845. The church celebrated its 150th birthday in 1995. A major extension to the original church was opened by the Bishop of Aston, Colin Buchanan in 1987 and a continued internal building project co-ordinated by the Reverend Barry Harper, to cater for increased numbers in the congregation, has since been completed.

New Shipton Farm. The age of New Shipton Farm is uncertain although the name is recorded in 1472 as Shippton. New Shipton Farm is mentioned in 1547 and the buildings are marked on the site on Yates' map of Warwickshire dated 1793. The existing farmhouse probably dates from the eighteenth or nineteenth century.

New Shipton Barn. Although not much to look at from the outside a surprise awaits inside. The barn is in fact a timber-framed cruck barn dating back to around 1435. One of the best examples of its type in Birmingham, it became a Grade II listed building in 1988.

The cruck-beamed barn. The oldest visible structure on the site is a four bay cruck-framed barn with all five pairs of cruck trusses surviving. The site has recently received planning permission to be converted into a restaurant and bar.

New Hall Mill, 1895.

Opposite: The mill and cottage before restoration, 1971. In 1897 a loaf of bread made from wheat which had been cut, threshed, ground and baked all on the same day, was sent to Queen Victoria to celebrate her Jubilee. The same feat was repeated in 1977 for our present Queen. Both loaves of bread are still in the royal collections.

New Hall Mill before restoration, 1971. There has been a mill at New Hall since at least the last quarter of the sixteenth century, and perhaps many years before. Improvements to the mill seem to have been made in the 1850s. This could be when the external waterwheel was moved to its present position to replace one of the two internal wheels. It seems likely that there were two waterwheels at the mill from the earliest buildings until the late nineteenth century.

New Hall Mill, 1989. In 1970 Sir Alfred Owen, owner of the New Hall Estate, decided to restore the mill to working order. Due to problems of the water supply the mill had ceased milling with water power around 1960, although a diesel engine was installed so milling did not cease completely. A survey was carried out in 1971 and work to restore the mill was undertaken. The New Hall Mill Preservation Trust was established in 1973 and leased the mill from Rubery Owen and Company Limited, with the aim of ensuring its future.

The stone floor which contains two pairs of millstones. After the death of the last miller, Ben Davis, further work in 1991 and 1996 was carried out and along with members of the Midland Wind and Watermills Group, the mill was prepared for official reopening on 12 May 1996. The Friends of New Hall Mill was formed and members work with the Trust to maintain and develop the site, as well as operating the machinery on open days.

The garner (attic floor). Grain was stored in sacks on the top floor and tipped into chutes or bins which led down to the stones or other milling machines. The chains of the sack hoist, which can be seen in the centre of the photograph, are used for lifting the sacks of grain from the ground floor to the garner floor on the second level.

Ford keeper's cottage, 1992, one of the fifty-one stone cottages built during Bishop Vesey's time. The houses, although varying in size, are all of one type; they were built with quions at angles and with door and windows of well dressed stone. The roofs appear always to have been meant for tiles. A particularly interesting feature about the Vesey Houses is the spiral stone staircase; it is always placed in the wall at or near the angle, and not far from the doorway.

New Hall Valley, looking to New Shipton on the footpath from Walmley Road, 1994. As far back as 1994, Birmingham City Council and many local people wished to 'open up' the New Hall Valley for public use and enjoyment. It was hoped that this could be achieved by designating the area as a Country Park.

New Hall Valley; the footpath from Warren House Farm to New Hall Mill, 1994. In 1997 the long awaited agreement for the new Country Park was signed between the land owners and the council.

The Ebrook, New Hall Valley, 1994. The Ebrook, or Plantsbrook as it known today, powered many of Sutton Coldfield's water mills. It rises in Sutton Park and flows through the centre of Sutton, through New Hall Valley to Plantsbrook Nature Reserve and into the River Tame at Castle Bromwich.

New Hall Valley, looking from Wylde Green Road to Bishop Walsh School, 1992. The New Hall Valley of some 250 acres contains various features including an area of wetlands in the north of the site which is of exceptional interest, both for plants and bird life.

Warren House Farm, which possibly dates from about 1530 and is one of the Bishop Vesey houses. Much altered, the rough-cast walls on the western side are inscribed 1671. It was most probably built as a farmhouse.

New Hall from the 1882 sales catalogue. This describes New Hall as 'a very valuable and important freehold residential property known as 'New Hall'; comprising of a noble mansion with charming pleasure grounds and gardens, also with two farms with houses and homesteads and 407 acres of finely timbered land, possessing extensive frontage to main roads.'

Sales catalogue of New Hall, 28 July 1882.

PARTICULARS.

LOT 1.
(Coloured Blue on Plan.)

THE IMPORTANT AND BEAUTIFUL

FREEHOLD ESTATE

KNOWN AS

"NEW HALL,"

IN THE

PARISH OF SUTTON COLDFIELD,

WARWICKSHIRE,

Situate about a mile from the Town and the same distance from Penn and Sutton Coldfield Stations of Midland Railway, seven miles by road from Birmingham, and nine and a half from Lichfield.

IT COMPRISES A

Grand Old Family Mansion,

Most Substantially Built in the Tudor Style,

PLEASANTLY PLACED ON AN ELEVATED POSITION,

SURROUNDED BY

A MOAT OF CLEAR SPRING WATER,

IN THE MIDST OF

CHARMING GROUNDS,

TASTEFULLY LAID-OUT AND OF GREAT NATURAL BEAUTY,

WITH

SHRUBBERIES AND ROOKERY,

OVERLOOKING

UNDULATING AND PARK-LIKE LAND,

INTERSECTED BY

A TROUT STREAM

AND BORDERED BY

ORNAMENTAL WOODS & PLANTATIONS.

New Hall Hotel, 1992. New Hall dates back to around 1200. The building is, in effect, built in four sections, the left side being the early section, the middle being Elizabethan, the right Victorian and, off the picture, the modern 1992 extension.

Entrance to New Hall Hotel, 1992. Work began in 1986 on a £3 million conversion of New Hall to transform it into a top class hotel. The house and 2 acres were sold to the Thistle Hotel Group in 1985.

New Hall Hotel extension, 1992. The construction of fifty-one bedrooms in a new block was designed to be in keeping with the hall's architectural style. Managed by Mr and Mrs Parkes, the hotel has since had many famous people as its guests and has won many top awards.

Langley Hall, 1981. The hall is thought to have been built in the thirteenth century. It was demolished early in the nineteenth century, but Langley Hall Farm, the outbuildings of the house, survived.

Langley Hall, 1981. The old stable block, built around 1685, became derelict for more than ten years. In 1987 the hall was sold by the Langley Charitable Trust to Vandelta Homes.

Langley Hall being converted into luxury homes. Situated on Ox Leys Road, the seventeenth century listed building was restored and converted into twelve luxury homes in 1988, each with their own gardens, and set around a landscaped communal courtyard.

Langley Hall moat. Langley Hall was one of several buildings in the area which were moated. This is all that remains of the moat today.

Langley Gorse, Fox Hollies Road. Shown on the 1856 Valuation Map of Sutton Coldfield, Langley Gorse was once the home of the famous eventing horse woman Janet Hodgson, who took part in the 1973 European Championships at Kiev.

The Grove, Wishaw. Possibly one of the oldest houses in Sutton Coldfield, this must have been a house in which some important individual lived. Who it was is not known, but the house had probably been built when the Lay Sudsidy Roll was made in 1332. The buildings are cruck-built dwellings and are one of the earliest types of construction.

Walmley Ash Road, August 1980. Plans as far back as 1976 were put forward to build on land between Walmley Ash Road and Fox Hollies Road. One of the largest housing schemes in Birmingham at the time, Bi-Vis (Holdings) Limited planned to build 1,400 homes on 124 acres of land at Oak Farm, on Walmley Ash Road, with another 27 acres left for open space.

The Chase, off Fox Hollies Road, August 1980.

Seven
Minworth and Wiggins Hill

The Birmingham Fazeley Canal bursts its banks at Kingsbury Road, Minworth, from Saturday to Sunday 16-17 March 1947.

The Hare and Hounds public house, date unknown.

Minworth Cottages, Kingbury Road. The cottages were demolished in 1960.

Minworth Green, April 1959.

The Hare and Hounds public house from across the Green, May 1959.

Cottage Lane.

Tudor Farm House, Wiggins Hill, 1910. This may be one of three messuages spoken of as existing in 1570.

Tudor Farm House.

The Old Meeting House. (The burial ground was between the garden and the house.) Wiggins Hill has no church but in 1724 the Society of Friends built a meeting house there. The Quakers' place of worship was described as 'a homely little meeting house with an adjoining cottage.' The cost of the building was a little over £100, £40 of which was raised by collections within the county. However, within a few years the Quaker congregation began to dwindle in numbers, and the meeting house finally closed after serving its purpose for a little over a century.

Eight

Sutton Park

Aerial view of Sutton Park, facing north, showing Wyndley, Keepers, Blackroot and Bracebridge Pools.

Sutton Park from a drawing by J.D. Harding and engraved by W. Radcliffe, 1827.

Agnes Bracken sketch of Sutton Park, 1854. Agnes Bracken was born in Erdington in November 1800. Her family moved to Sutton Coldfield in 1816 and in 1820 she moved into the High Street. She was a teacher by profession, but was also an artist.

Looking towards Sutton's parish church in a sketch by Agnes Bracken. Her views of Sutton and its environs are not only valuable as works of art, but also as records of scenes now gone. She is also noted for her work on the history of Sutton Coldfield published as *The Forest and Chase of Sutton Coldfield*.

A sketch of Sutton Park by Agnes Bracken, who died in 1877. Holbeche describes her as 'A women first, authoress, artist, antiquarian, philanthropist, of the strongest individuality, with the softest of hearts.'

Park Road and Town Gate, which were constructed in 1826 when William Hartop exchanged land ownership with the Corporation.

The shelter near Town Gate. The Council minutes of February 1951 report that the Borough Surveyor had submitted plans for the construction of a shelter near the main gate. At the meeting of 11 June the Surveyor reported that the construction of this shelter had been completed.

Park House, *c.* 1870, before the alterations of 1898. Park House stands in its own grounds within Sutton Park. Today it is used as a restaurant but in the days of Elizabeth I it had an entirely different purpose. It was Sutton's first blade mill, the first Sutton mill to employ a tilt hammer, which was used to shape metal into blades. The buildings were extensively altered in 1898.

Park House after alterations. In 1948 Sutton Coldfield Corporation purchased the property for £18,250 which consisted of 19 acres including pools and woods. Today it is a restaurant.

Wyndley Lane, March 1964. One of the oldest roads in Sutton Coldfield, it cut through solid sandstone and provided a route from the town via Manor Hill and Driffold to Sutton Park. Before the Park was formed, Wyndley Lane provided access to the deer park from the Manor.

Wyndley Gate, June 1964. Until the construction of Park Road and Town Gate in 1826, Wyndley Lane was the only entrance for traffic into the Park.

The Refreshment Shed, Wyndley Pool, 1893. A café on Wyndley Pool which readers may well remember, was closed on 23 September 1973. The café, run by Mr Arthur Henry Adderly and his mother Mrs Elsie Wellsbury, offered refreshments there from 1952. After failing to reach an agreement over the lease with the Sutton Council it was closed in 1973.

Wyndley Pool Cottage, *c.* 1900.

Wyndley Pool. Although classed as the oldest pool in the Park - the pool is first recorded during the reign of Henry V (1413-1422) - it was not until 1937 that the pool actually became part of Sutton Park, when the Somerville Trust transferred 152 acres of land to the Corporation for the building of Monmouth Drive, and additional land for the inclusion into Sutton Park.

Rowing boats on Wyndley Pool. An advertisement in Sidwell and Durant's Guide of 1900 states that Wyndley was under new management. A new fleet of fifty boats and canoes were for hire. Boating from 6.00 to 9.00 in the morning was half price. Good fishing with the use of a punt was 2s 6d per day; from the side it was 1s 6d; half day fishing for the season was £1 1s. Today no fishing is allowed as the pool is a wildlife reserve.

Crystal Palace, May 1962. The Crystal Palace was opened in 1868. The scheme was started by a market gardener who began by opening up his grounds to the public. The idea snowballed and the Crystal Palace became a favourite haunt for locals and day-trippers from Birmingham. Originally a hotel was built along side the Palace and there were stables to accommodate fifty horses. For the general public there were 30 acres of grassland.

Crystal Palace dome, 1962. The Zoological Gardens, which were opened at the turn of the century, offered special attractions such as monkeys, lions, bears, wolves, leopards, camels, antelopes, kangaroos and hundreds of other novelties. The Palace catered for 1,500 persons under cover and offered dinners, teas and other refreshments on the most 'liberal terms'.

89

Crystal Palace, 1962. The famous showman Pat Collins took over the Crystal Palace around 1910. In the early 1960s the Palace buildings deteriorated and unfortunately it was demolished in May 1962. The Clifton Road Youth Centre stands on the site today.

Hollyhurst. One of seven of the early wooded enclosures, Hollyhurst takes its name from the holly which was the most dominant tree of that area.

The White House, Hollyhurst, January 1941. It was from here that the free holly issued to the residents of Sutton was collected. The house was built in about 1826. An advertisement in the 1900 guide quotes, 'Charles Townshend refreshment contractor. Dinners, teas and refreshments of the best quality, at the most moderate prices. Best accommodation in Sutton Park for schools and large parties. Good shelter for 1,000 persons.'

Sutton Park Visitor Centre, 1989. Designed by students from the University of Central England, the visitors' centre in Sutton Park, costing £145,000, was opened in May 1985. Situated between Town Gate and Wyndley Gate, it houses comprehensive displays on the history and wildlife in Sutton Coldfield's outstanding landscape.

Boldmere Gate.

Powells Pool. Keepers guard the
bank after drowning fatalities
occurred on 8 August 1937.

The sign erected after the drowning
fatalities at Powells Pool on 8
August 1937.

Aldermen Pearson unveiling the Boldmere Swimming Club War Memorial in Sutton Park, near Powells Pool, 1921. The memorial was originally erected on what was known as Hallets Field overlooking Powells Pool near the Boldmere entrance. The statue was sculptured by Ben Creswick who lived in Jockey Road. The plinth on which the statue stood had on it all the names of Boldmere Swimming Club members who died in the First World War. It was unveiled by the Mayor on 29 October 1921. The statue, without its plinth, was moved to stand outside Wyndley Swimming Baths when they opened in 1974.

Powells Pool Pavilion after alterations which were completed in December 1939. Sutton Coldfield Corporation took over the management of Powells Pool Pavilion in June 1949 and it was in daily use as a café, providing lunches and teas.

Powells Pool Pavilion interior, 1949. Extensive cloakrooms were added during the summer and the hall was used for dances, concerts, lectures and meetings. The hall was licensed for singing and dancing until 11.00 pm. The main hall was 70 feet long by 30 feet wide and 160 persons could dance in comfort.

The National Fire Service camp. Previously used and built by the Home Office for a Civil Defence camp during the Second World War, the camp stood near to Powells Pool.

Head keeper Smith of Rowton Cottage, date unknown.

Blackroot Pool, July 1995. 'In the year 1759, The Warden and Society agreed a Grant of Lease of 12 acres of ground, which was then a bog, to Mr Duncumb for 42 years at 2 shillings rent per annum in consideration that Mr Duncumb, at his own expense, make a pool or pond of water of the same... at his own proper costs and charge keep and maintain in good repair upon the dam and open Common Road or highway for cattle and all sorts and kinds whatsoever on foot and on horseback, to pass upon, over and along the same at all times without restraint.'

Logging near Keepers Pool, 1937. Logging has always played an important role in the conservation of Sutton Park. Today the wood from the trees is used for the repairing of the Park's fences. Figures for the number of trees felled in the eighteenth century show that in 1726, 5,784 trees were felled, in 1771, 536 and in 1786, just 60. Between 1726 and 1792 a total of 15,382 trees were cut down.

The opening of the shelter at Blackroot Hill

Four Oaks Gate. Up until 1974 when Sutton Coldfield became part of Birmingham, the residents of the Borough had free access to the Park, while those who lived outside the Borough had to pay an admission fee. Birmingham abolished the admission charge in 1974.

Hartop Gate. The 2,400 acre Park, given to the people of Sutton Coldfield by Henry VIII in 1528, famous for its wetlands, grasslands and lowlands, is Europe's largest urban park and boasts on average two million visitors a year. It was designated as a Site of Scientific Interest under the National Parks and Access to the Country Act (1949) in 1954 and was renotified in 1987 under the Wildlife and Countryside Act (1981). In April 1997 the Park received its new status. English Nature, the agency responsible for wildlife and nature conservation in England, awarded it the status of a National Nature Reserve. The Park is the only National Nature Reserve to be surrounded by urban development confirming that the Park is indeed the 'Jewel in the Crown.'

Nine
The Pageant and
The Jamboree

The Revd F.S. Golden as Bishop Vesey, and N.W. Kimberly as Henry VIII.

The Romans battle with the English on Icknield Street. In July 1928 The Royal Town of Sutton Coldfield celebrated the fourth century of the signing of the Charter given to the people by Henry VIII. To celebrate the event the residents of Sutton revived the pageantry of the history of Sutton and its people.

The 1928 Pageant, which was held in Sutton Park in the area known as Hollyhurst. Over 1,200 people took part in the event, watched by some 6,000 spectators. The historic narrative *Sutton Through the Centuries* was written by J.E. Willmott and The Pageant was directed by Henry Millar. It re-enacted scenes from the Roman times to the Victorians.

'Falstaff's Ragged Army Passes on its Way to Shrewsbury', Falstaff being played by E. Greenwood. Judging by the statements of accounts, The Pageant was a huge success. Admissions taken on the gates of the Park came to £2,307 18s 7d. The total amount made by the event was £2,866 5s 5d.

Victorian section of The Pageant. John Willmott, although offered the office of mayor, was unable to accept the position through business commitments; however he was made a Freeman of the Town and has a school named after him.

Scouts arriving at Sutton Park for the World Scout Jubilee Jamboree. This was a unique gathering of scouts from all parts of the world. It comprised of a World Scout Jamboree, a World Rover Moot and a World Scouters Indaba. Never before had the three events been held at the same place and at the same time. The Jamboree was a major world celebration of the Baden-Powell birthday centenary and the Golden Jubilee of the world wide movement he founded. The purpose of all the Jamborees, Rover Moots and Indabas was to provide an opportunity for the scouts of different countries to meet and make individual friendships, thereby strengthening the bond of the scout brotherhood.

Putting the finishing touches to the revolving globe which was to feature all the countries where scouting existed. It was in the summer of 1953 that the Boy Scouts International Conference decided to celebrate fifty years of scouting with the holding of a hitherto untried combined international gathering, and it was with great pride that the Boy Scouts Association of the United Kingdom accepted the invitation to organise the great Jubilee event. The first important step was to find a suitable place in which to stage the vast camp. A short list was drawn up and in 1954 the appointed selectors paid their memorable visit to Sutton Park, where the event was to become known as the J.I.M. The citizens of Sutton Coldfield were justifiably proud when the Park was chosen for the holding of the Jubilee Jamboree Indaba and Moot, the J.I.M.

A decorative welcome arch erected by the citizens of Sutton Coldfield at the Wylde Green boundary. Why Jamboree, Indaba and Moot? Jamboree was the name given by Baden-Powell to the first international gathering of scouts at Olympia in 1920. When asked 'why Jamboree?', Baden-Powell replied 'what else would you call it?' The word Jamboree is now known and understood the world over. Indaba means 'a gathering of the chiefs'. The first World Indaba was held at Gilwell Park, Essex in 1952. Moot was again Baden-Powell's suggestion. It comes from an old English word meaning 'a gathering of young men for discussion concerning the affairs of the community'.

Just inside Town Gate, the triumphal arch towered 60 feet above the ground and had a span of 50 feet. Over a period of more than two years a voluntary army of over 5,000 people was formed to organise the event. In the face of ever increasing costs of labour and materials and of repeated political and industrial tension at home and abroad, the organisers set their course. To ensure that the vast camp would be properly serviced and the participants adequately accommodated, fed and entertained, the organisers soon found they would face an expenditure of over £500,000. It would have been more but for the generosity of British firms and her Majesty's Government, who either loaned equipment or supplied materials at very reduced rates.

French disabled scouts arrive at Town Gate. The Jamboree was attended by 31,000 scouts from 85 countries. Many of those countries have now been renamed. They came from Aden (210), Australia (169), Barbados (30), Belgium (1,508), Brazil (59), Canada (1,470) Cuba (53), Germany (2,000), Hong Kong (21), Iran (114), Italy (1,651), Leeward Islands (4), Mexico (30), Sarawak (21), South Africa (380), United Kingdom (9,844), United States of America (1,759), United Nations (1), and many more.

Scouts arriving at Sutton Park station. British Rail undertook the bulk of the intricate travel arrangements. Over 1,000,000 visitors were to visit the Jamboree and BR arranged 266 special trains for them to arrive on and to take them away, and arranged 83 special trains over 2 days. Scouts also arrived in the United Kingdom by boat and 10 ports were used. Representatives from 22 countries arrived by plane, the largest air contingent being 1,390 Canadian scouts. Three scout masters from Brazil road tested a jeep to reach Sutton; the Iranian contingent drove their own buses overland passing through Turkey, Greece, Yugoslavia, Trieste, Italy and France, and 190 of the 830 strong Austrian contingent arrived by cycle and motorcycle.

The Duke of Gloucester touches down on the golf course adjoining the Jamboree Camp. The official opening ceremony took place on 1 August 1957 and was performed by the Duke of Gloucester, President of the British Boy Scouts Association. At 3.00 in the afternoon he declared the Jubilee Jamboree Indaba and Moot officially open to 30,000 scouts in formation and an estimated 100,000 spectators.

Crowds await the arrival of the Queen and Prince Philip the Duke of Edinburgh on The Parade. The Queen arrived in Sutton on 3 August. As Royal Patron of the British Boy Scout Association, she and Prince Philip, Patron of the Baden-Powell Scout Guild, spent six hours with the scouts in the Park after being welcomed to the town by the Mayor of Sutton Coldfield Councillor Mrs K.E. Smith.

The Queen and Prince Philip tour the Jamboree Camp. During their visit the Royal guests spent much of their time on a six mile tour of the seven sub-camps. A parade of the Nations in the arena and the United Kingdom Air Scouts provided a spectacular display. An extract from the Queen's message following her visit to Sutton Park reads, 'They were heartened and delighted with the unforgettable welcome which they received from Scouts, Scouters and Rovers of many Nations... It was this which made their day at Sutton Park such a rewarding and enjoyable experience...'

Crowds disperse in Mill Street after the arrival of the Queen.

Crowds disperse on The Parade after the arrival of the Queen.

Sutton Coldfield's Mayor and the Lord Mayor and Lady Mayoress of Birmingham at a pig roasting at the Canadian sub-camp. The food bill for The Jamboree came to £160,000. During the 12 days 2,170,000 individual meals were prepared by the scouts themselves, in addition to snacks. Here are a few examples of what appeared on the gigantic shopping list: 40 tons of fresh meat, 486,600 eggs, 540,000 pints of milk, 432,000 bread rolls, 274,000 large loaves of bread, 16 tons of butter, 31 tons of sausages, 40 tons of sugar, $4\frac{1}{2}$ tons of tea, 14 tons of coffee, 40,500 bottles of sauces, 40 tons of fresh fruit and 15 cwt of prunes.

The Prime Minister Harold MacMillan tours the site on 10 August. The camp had all the amenities of a medium sized town. The camp centre comprised of a shopping area supplying everything the scout needed from a tent peg to a newspaper, to an aspirin. The site had 7 banks and its own telephone exchange, telephone number Jubilee 7711. To ensure an adequate supply of water (500,000 gallons a day was needed) huge water tanks with a total capacity of 250,000 gallons were erected on 30 ft high towers. More than 20 miles of pipeline were laid. Each sub-camp had its own medical inspection room and a first aid post. The camp hospital was loaned and erected by the Royal Air Force and contained 300 beds in 10 wards; a mobile dental clinic was also stationed in the Park. The camp had its own refuse collection vehicle and an SOS for the loan of 1,200 dustbins was answered. The site also had its own scout police and fire services.

Aerial view of The Jamboree. The police force was responsible for traffic control, safe guarding of property, the detailing of special traffic arrangements for the reception of VIPs and for generally maintaining order.

Gateway to the Moisson Camp. A fully equipped press camp was kept busy with accommodation for the press, radio and television. A 16 mm colour and sound film recording of The Jamboree was taken and is available for loan on video from Sutton Coldfield Reference Library.

Gateway to Vogelenzang. A 12-16 page daily newspaper was published entitled *Jubilee Journal*. The eleven editions cost 6d each. An estimated circulation of 40,000 inside the camp alone kept the scout newsboys busy delivering the editions in time for breakfast each morning.

Flags of the countries represented at The Jamboree. The General Post Office issued three special postage stamps to commemorate the event. It was the first time that Great Britain had issued a special stamp for a World Scout Jamboree. The stamps cost $2\frac{1}{2}$d for inland letter rate, 4d for foreign letter rate and 1s 3d for normal air mail letter rate.

Lady Baden-Powell closes The Jamboree on 12 August 1957. The great assembly at the closing ceremony was in great contrast to the one seen at the official opening twelve days earlier. All spectators and every scout flocked to the arena until it was filled to capacity. Lady Baden-Powell's words 'the end is only the beginning', ended the 1957 Jubilee Jamboree.

Ten
Sutton Coldfield Centre

The Parade, *c.* 1960s.

Lichfield Road, numbers 4, 6 and 8. Little is known of their histories. By 1850 the building had certainly been divided into three cottages and was in the possession of Edmund Perkins. In 1871 Perkins still owned the property and his tenants were William Yates, John Cook and Richard Bromwich. The buildings were demolished in August 1963.

The High Street, 1960s. The building occupied by Dixon, Dobson and Carver was, in the late 1800s, the home of Mr and Mrs Pratt. Mr Pratt was a very stout and heavy man and when he died they were unable to get his coffin downstairs and through the door. So they had to push it out through the upstairs bedroom window and precariously lower it to the hearse waiting in the street below. After his death his widow supported herself by selling sweetmeats and sparkling lemon pop.

112

The High Street, showing The Royal and The Three Tuns. In January 1975 Allied Breweries submitted plans to demolish the buildings on either side of The Three Tuns and build a car park and offices between High Street, Railway Road and King Edward Square. The plans were rejected. In February 1977 the buildings were demolished. However it was not until 1982 that King Edward Court, containing six individual units, was built and completed.

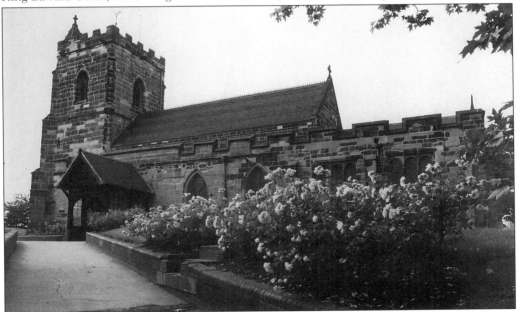

Holy Trinity Church, 1992. Despite strong opposition from local residents, plans to build a new community centre and car park in the church grounds and graveyard went ahead. Human remains were removed and work started on the centre in December 1994. The £1.4 million centre was officially opened on 11 May 1996.

Mill Street from the corner of Coleshill Street, May 1968.

Mill Street, May 1968. Mill Street takes its name from the mill which stood at the bottom of the road near to where the library stands today. Some of the old cottages were demolished on Mill Street in the early 1970s. In 1983 the owners of the area on the western side of the street, Emmanual College, were looking to redevelop the site.

Mill Street looking towards the High Street, July 1992. The old buildings were demolished and after an archaeological dig on the site in 1989 which unearthed evidence of fourteenth, seventeenth and eighteenth century buildings, work on the £5.8 million office complex commenced. Emmanual Court consisted of a 42,000 sq ft courtyard which incorporated the frontages of two of the old buildings, the old post office and the gatehouse. The eleven two storey and three storey unit designs were stepped to cope with the step fall of the land.

The opening of the Borough Restaurant on South Parade, 1942.

Park Road, *c.* 1910, looking towards the railway bridge from Sutton Park to the town centre.

116

Park Road looking towards the railway bridge. The corner of Railway Road is on the left. The houses on the right were demolished in October 1963.

Park Road at the corner of Station Street and Mill Street before Brassington Avenue was built, May 1972. Brassington Avenue, named after a past Mayor of Sutton, was built across the dry bed of the old mill pond. It was built in the early 1990s as a ring road for the Gracechurch Centre.

Birmingham Road from opposite The Cup, looking towards The Parade, *c.* 1949.

Queen Street, numbers 13-19, January 1995.

Newhall Street. The first edition 25 inch Ordnance Survey map of 1887 shows Newhall Street as only having ten houses on it. By the second edition of 1903 there are twenty-eight houses.

Newhall Street, July 1992. In the 1990s the houses were sold to MEPC who bought them from a private landlord. The houses were leased to Sharpe Housing Association on short term leases and demolished in 1994. Although the road was lost with the new development, its name is remembered with the name of the new shopping area - New Hall Walk.

The Wesleyan Church on The Parade before it was converted into the library, *c*. 1930. This church, on the corner of Newhall Street, was opened in 1887 to a packed congregation in the year of Queen Victoria's Golden Jubilee. The builder was Mr Simons of Aston. The Mayor, Benjamin Stone, laid the foundation stone on 10 September 1887. The building cost £1,675 to build.

The opening of Sutton Coldfield Library, 6 March 1937. On 30 October 1935 Sutton Council reported that they had agreed the sum of £7,200 for the purchase of the church and in February 1936, the Council became its new owners. The building alterations cost £4,864 and a further £6,500 was spent on furnishings and books. The library opened to the public in March 1937.

Sutton Coldfield Central Library, 1960. Although plans to redevelop the area where the library stood were put forward in 1988, the revised plans in 1994 provoked strong local protests. A group was set up to try and save the Old Library Centre from demolition. Used for community purposes, the protests failed to save the building and it was demolished in February 1995.

Lower Parade and the Empress Cinema, *c.* 1950s. The cinema did not escape the earlier redevelopment of the 1970s. It had opened on 1 January 1923 showing *East is West* starring Constance Tolmadge. In 1935 it had a new stage, balcony and projection suite, but it finally closed its doors on 2 January 1971 after showing *Jane Eyre*.

The Parade, 1948.

The Parade and Lower Parade, 1948.

The Parade looking towards Mill Street, 1960s.

The Parade, 1960s. The building used as Woolworth's had previously been the Picture House Cinema, costing a penny downstairs and tuppence upstairs. After Woolworth's moved into the Gracechurch Centre on the other side of the road, the building opened as Sutton Coldfield's Market Hall. A fire in 1993 destroyed the building.

The Parade, 1960s. The Parade seems to have suffered with traffic congestion over the centuries. In the mid 1800s it is recorded that twenty coaches passed through the centre daily at a rate of ten miles an hour.

The Parade, 1960s. In was in the '60s that Sutton Council started to look at the western side of The Parade with a view to redevelopment. With the building of the Gracechurch Centre, Sutton centre lost many of its attractive shops, the buildings of which, although they had changed names, had altered little since the early part of the century.

The Gracechurch Centre, November 1974. In 1969 plans were finalised and the developers, the United Kingdom Provident Institution, set about redeveloping the 7 acres of land. It took 5 years to build and the centre took its name from the developer's head office, Gracechurch Street, London. Constructed by John Lang it cost £7 million to build. The complex, containing some 4,500,000 bricks, 100,000 metric tons of concrete and 5,000 metric tons of reinforcing steel was opened by the Earl of Aylesford on 4 December 1974.

The Gracechurch Centre and Plantsbrook House with Sutton's old boundary sign, July 1992. The year 1996 saw refurbishment work start on the centre. The old boundary sign and gardens have been replaced by the space age circular building The Café Rouge, which opened on 26 March 1997. The £8.2 million project marked the twenty-second birthday of the Gracechurch Centre and the new tented structure makes it one of the most contemporary buildings in Sutton Coldfield.

The Parade, July 1992. Plans by MEPC Developments were put forward for 'The Royal Parades' in 1988. Revised plans in 1994 were strongly opposed. The site from Lower Queen Street to South Parade meant the loss of Newhall Street and the moving of Plantsbrook Stream. The new designs, which included eleven shops, four retail warehouses, a restaurant and a 240 space car park, were completed in 1996.

The Parade from Newhall Street looking to Queen Street, 1995. The Parade Buildings were built in 1884. The end building, No. 83, was occupied for many years by Fawdry Brothers, bakers and corn merchants, and then by Bourne and Sons. Number 87 was a butchers and No. 85 was occupied by Richard Stevetons, a gas fitter.

The Parade, numbers 89-95, January 1995. Attempts were made to save these buildings, designed by Crouch, Butler and Savage and built in 1908 and 1910, from demolition, by getting them put on the list of nationally listed buildings. Unfortunately there had been too many alterations over the years for them to be included. They were demolished in May 1995.

The Parade looking from Queen Street, July 1992.

The start of the demolition of The Parade, February 1995. Despite all the protests, planning permission was granted to MEPC in 1995 for the revised but ambitious redevelopment project. The developers did listen to some of the protesters and Plantsbrook Stream, instead of being buried under the new car park, was moved to the edge of Queen Street and made a feature of the new area.

View from Sainbury's car park looking to what is left of Newhall Street and Queen Street, 1995. In that year demolition started and the site was cleared of the buildings from the late 1880s and early 1900s, leaving it ready for the next stage in Sutton Coldfield's history.